Native American Herbalism

The Ultimate Herbal Encyclopedia
With Theory

(A Complete Medical Handbook of Native American Herbs)

Helaine White

Published By **Bella Frost**

Helaine White

All Rights Reserved

Native American Herbalism: The Ultimate Herbal Encyclopedia With Theory (A Complete Medical Handbook of Native American Herbs)

ISBN 978-1-77485-847-9

No part of this guidebook shall be reproduced in any form without permission in writing from the publisher except in the case of brief quotations embodied in critical articles or reviews.

Legal & Disclaimer

The information contained in this ebook is not designed to replace or take the place of any form of medicine or professional medical advice. The information in this ebook has been provided for educational & entertainment purposes only.

The information contained in this book has been compiled from sources deemed reliable, and it is accurate to the best of the Author's knowledge; however, the Author cannot guarantee its accuracy and validity and cannot be held liable for any errors or omissions. Changes are periodically made to this book. You must consult your doctor or get professional medical advice before using any of the suggested remedies, techniques, or information in this book.

Upon using the information contained in this book, you agree to hold harmless the Author from and against any damages, costs, and expenses, including any legal fees potentially resulting from the application of any of the information provided by this guide. This disclaimer applies to any damages or injury caused by the use and application, whether directly or indirectly, of any advice or information presented, whether for breach of contract, tort, negligence, personal injury, criminal intent, or under any other cause of action.

You agree to accept all risks of using the information presented inside this book. You need to consult a professional medical practitioner in order to ensure you are both able and healthy enough to participate in this program.

Table Of Contents

Chapter 1: Modern Native American Medicaline 1

Chapter 2: How To Store And Source Herbs 19

Chapter 3: Herbal Preparations 29

Chapter 4: Native American Medicinal Plants 43

Chapter 1: Modern Native American Medicaline

All over the world, ative Americans have been known for their medicinal knowledge. Rumour has it that there are about 200 Native American herbs in every 400 drugs you'll find. Many modern medications contain active ingredients made from Native American herbs, such as ginger, echinacea, ampalaya and ginger. They're used in drug therapy, but you can also find them in beauty products, hair oils, and other such items.

Oral history says that Native American herbalism began over 10,000 years ago. Unfortunately, there is no reliable historical documentation that documents the activities of Native American tribes until they come into contact the Europeans in about 16 century. We have now only the orally transmitted systems and beliefs, passed down through generations.

There is one story, however, that I find particularly interesting among the numerous oral stories told by the natives. This is a story about the Native Americans discovering the healing power of herbs. It is said that the natives became interested in herbalism after watching animals. They discovered the magical properties of herbs and roots by watching how the animals that they observed quickly recovered from illness after having consumed some herbs.

While you might find this story unbelievable, there are some truths to it. If you are familiar with American natives, you will be able to see how strong they are in "reasoning from verification." This is what Western philosophers term empiricism (i.e. the belief that knowledge can only come from experience). This story can be supported by another explanation: Their apparent dependence upon plains, forests, and coastal areas.

Native Americans do not like to share their traditional herb knowledge with nonnative Americans due to the way that some people have dismissed their herbalism. Native

American Medicine has enjoyed a worldwide popularity due to this generosity.

Native American Herbs Have Medicinal Properties

It is vital that you read through these healing agents together so you have a complete understanding of how they work.

The healing properties of plants come from their natural components. Modern medicine now recognizes these elements as minerals and vitamins, phytochemicals, enzymes, and other nutrients. I've been talking endlessly about the medicinal benefits of native American herbal herbs since the beginning. You may have wondered, "What are these herbal medicinal capabilities?" In this section we will examine each of them individually. Learn the healing properties of American Native herbs.

Phytochemicals

Since "phyto", which means plants, phytochemicals could also be called "plant chemicals". When consumed, these chemicals act as antioxidants and immune system strengthening agents, enzyme release stimulants, plaque destruction in blood vessels, etc.

Below are some of these plant chemicals which are extremely concentrated in native American plants:

* Alkaloids

This group has the most medicinal properties. It will always be present in some plant. They can be found in nearly every food, drink, or supplement we consume. They include neuroactive molecules like nicotine or caffeine, which are commonplace ingredients in our daily lives. You'll also find vinblastine, vincristine, and emetine in many native American species. Nightshades and goldenseal are two plants high in alkaloids. They help eliminate toxic substances from the body, strengthen our defense system, and aid in detox.

* Anthocyanins

Anthocyanins (natural pigments) are natural dyes that create new colors in plants, vegetables and fruits. Anthocyanins make up a large percentage of any herb found in blue, violet, a red/purple color, purple or violet. Echinacea, one of the most used and loved native American herbs in America, has high amounts of anthocyanins.

Anthocyanins help build the body's defense against free-radicals. These substances are created after metabolic reactions have been triggered. This material can cause serious conditions such cancer or cardiovascular disease.

Anthocyanins prevent the formation plaques in the bloodstream and stabilize blood flow. This helps to reduce the risk of developing coronary disease. They can also improve your vision and fight edema.

* Chlorophyll

While we all know the function and benefits of chlorophyll in plants, many don't know what this plant resource can do for us as humans. The plant's greenness is caused by chlorophyll. It aids in photosynthesis by absorbing sunlight.

Chlorophyll is a different kind of plant. It:

* Reduces the risk of infection by bacteria

* can be used to treat burns and other wounds.

* Helps to fight cancer

* is a great place to get vitamin K. Vitamin K improves the skin and helps strengthen bones.

* Diterpenes

Diterpenes can be found in almost all herbal plants. Bertoni (and Rosemary) are potent detoxifiers and anti-inflammatory agents.

* Eleutherosides

Are you looking to boost your energy or improve your overall health? If you are looking for energy, then any plant that contains high amounts of eleutherosides could be a good option. Follow the instructions carefully and follow them as directed. The effects will increase your stamina as well as mental alertness.

Eleutherosides increase your appetite and immune system. They also stimulate body metabolism. It is commonly used to treat irregular periods and hot flashes in menopause.

* Essential Fatty Acids

There are just two essential oils. These are: omega-3 fatty acid (alpha-linolenic Acid) and omega-6 fatty acid (linoleic Acid). Other types of fatty acids are considered "conditionally necessary" since they become essential only when certain diseases or events occur.

These essential fatty oils are crucial for good health. However, the body is unable to break them down. To get these vital fatty acids, we need to consume these herbs.

Below are the functions they perform inside the body.

* They ensure that the cell membranes (nerve fibers cover) and myelin sheds (cell membranes) are in proper shape.

* They stimulate hormone-like substances, called prostaglandin. These substances boost immunity and accelerate your metabolism.

They are also known to improve nerve transmission and stimulate muscle activity.

They are found in many herbs but the most common is the palmetto.

* Flavonglycosides

This plant chemical can be used as an antioxidant. It removes plaques from blood vessels and improves blood flow. Flavonglycosides, a powerful antidepressant, is also available. Ginkgo biloba can supply this substance.

* Gingerols

Gingerols can be described as an active component in ginger. This is the herb substance that improves digestion. Consuming gingerol-rich plants will make your digestive system work much more efficiently to help you break down fats, proteins, as well as transfer nutrients to every body part. This antioxidant can also combat liver toxicity.

* Ginkolic Acid

Another powerful antioxidant that is found in Native American herbal remedies is this.

Imagine a multiple-in-one package. This is what the plant chemical is. It improves blood circulation, mental clarity, reduces the risk of getting degenerative diseases and fights cancer.

It's also a great way to reduce depression. It can also help with depression.

* Glycyrrhizins

This chemical compound is typically extracted from licorice. It is often used in skin-care products because of its anti-inflammatory properties, antiviral and repair properties.

* Hesperidin

Hesperidin helps strengthen your cells and protect your capillaries. Hesperidin can also be used to treat liver diseases like cirrhosis, hepatitis, and others. Hesperidin provides protection from damaging light rays, and can be obtained from milk thistle plants.

* Hypericin

Hypericin is an antibiotic/antivirus/anti-depressant derivative of St. John's wort. This substance controls neurotransmitters in our mind and has been used throughout the years for anxiety, depression, and sleeping disorders.

* Isothiocyanates

Another common plant chemical extracted from Native American plants is isothiocyanates. Horseradish is a good source of Isothiocyanates. They stimulate protective enzymes and protect DNA. This helps reduce cancer risk in any area of the body. They are especially well-known for their ability to prevent cancer. Isothiocyanates can prevent carcinogenesis as well as facilitate detoxification. Recent research on this compound has also shown that they fight tumors.

* Lactones

Isothiocyanates also have anticarcinogenic properties. They can reduce the chance of developing cancer. They also have been shown to be skin sensitive and can be obtained from the root of kava kava.

* Lipoic Acid

Lipoic Acid is a powerful antioxidant found in many herbs. This substance is known to inhibit the growth and elimination of metals. It is effective in reducing skin roughness, reducing cancer risk, and keeping blood sugar in check. They are effective in relieving inflammation, tiredness, heart disease, and memory loss.

* Phenolic acid

Fruits, seeds, and fruit skins can contain phenolic acids. But, plants, especially those from the USA, have high concentrations of these compounds. This acid is rich antioxidants that prevent cancer, inhibit oxidative stresses and reduce oxidative damage. It can also help with heart disease and diabetes. These substances can be found in parsley, berries, and most other plants.

* Phthalides

Phthalides are excellent detoxifiers from carcinogens. Phthalides are found in many drugs as they relax blood vessels to lower blood pressure and increase blood flow. Phthalides can also be used to ensure the production of essential enzymes necessary for good health.

* Polyacetylenes

The body produces carcinogens and prostaglandins by using polyacetylenes.

* Proanthocyanidins

Proanthocyanins can protect you from cancer, improve blood vessel strength and balance your cholesterol. They also act as an antioxidant to fight the influenza virus. These are found in elderberry and bilberry.

* Quercetin

Quercetin can be found in many fruits and vegetables. Flavonoids can be described as a class of antioxidants found in plants. They are well-known for their ability to protect cells membranes and blood vessels from injury and provide anti-inflammation and cancer properties.

* Rosmarinic Acid

You've probably heard of this type of acid before. They are very popular and often are the active ingredients in many modern medications we take.

They were extracted from rosemary and used in drug production to improve digestion and fight nausea. This phytochemical may also be effective in treating mild pains, such as headaches.

* Salin

Hippocrates recommended white willow barks, leaves and other herbal medicines to his patients. This plant also contains salicin, a phytochemical known as salt. This compound is ingested to help with inflammation, pain and fever. It is highly effective in the treatment of the influenza virus.

* Saponins

Saponins have been used as cough syrups, emetics and sneezing pills. This is because they help remove phlegm. They are activated immediately by our cholesterin which means they can only be effective on our mucus membrane. They're great anti-cancer agent.

* Silymarin

Another phytochemical, this one is derived form milk thistle. It is a powerful antioxidant and helps ensure optimal liver function.

* Tannins

Tannins occur in almost every plant. They are antioxidants as well as antiviral substances that can improve your capillary performance, lower your risk of cancer, asthma, heart disease, and other diseases in your body.

* Terpenes

Terpenes, the chemical responsible to the cannabis plant's smell, are also known as terpenes. You can find them in Ginkgo biloba. They are also great for your health. They are antioxidants when consumed regularly. They also have therapeutic effects comparable to cannabinoids, such as CBD or THC.

* Triterpenoids

Getu Kola and licorice root can be used to treat and prevent ulcers. These plants are rich sources of triterpenoids. They can also be used to treat dental decay.

Enzymes

Enzymes, which are "catalysts," of phytochemicals, are responsible for generating them. They are required for the body to function properly. They are necessary for the smooth absorption the other properties of herbs. These enzymes are necessary for you to be healthy. For the best results, it is important to ensure that your remedy does not come in contact with alcohol or extreme heat.

Benefits and Uses

Although we already mentioned the many health benefits of native American herbs in our previous section, I feel it's important that we thoroughly go over them so you can fully understand the potential benefits.

Modern extraction techniques are being used to ensure that herbalism is fully harnessed.

Modern medicine still relies on herbal medicine as the basis for most of its components.

Native American herbs are useful for many things, and the benefits they offer are numerous. The current list of herbs is not complete and many more can be found in native America or elsewhere. It'd be helpful to understand some of the benefits of herbal medication, if not all.

Herbs are an excellent way to prevent cancer, heart disease, and other serious conditions that often require topical or regular medication. They are natural extracts that can be used fresh. This makes it easier to absorb the herbal properties of the medicine into our bodies, allowing them to serve their purpose effectively and ultimately improving your health.

Antioxidants are more concentrated in herbs that have been unmodified. When you consume herbs, your body will be able quickly harness their therapeutic effects, leading to a longer and healthier life.

Modern medicines often use different chemicals for preservation, which can lead to more adverse side effects than herbal treatments. However, side effects can be avoided with herbs. These herbs not only give you faster results but also help to reduce side effects.

Conclusion

Many native Americans didn't realize the medicinal properties that the herbs they ingested when they first used them. If you asked them today, they would likely not know. It's not because they didn't understand the herbs. They did. There was no easy way to know this information at that time. Their only concern was the fact that the herbs were effective and that they truly enjoyed their benefits.

If you look back at history, you will see that these indigenous people knew which herb to use when they were suffering from an illness.

This knowledge has proven to be very useful over the years. Rosemary is one example. They did not know the medicinal properties of rosemary or the healing agents that cause the headaches to subside.

Chapter 2: How To Store And Source Herbs
Gathering Herbs in the Right Way

Even though this sounds unbelievable, many people don't know where to source quality herbs. This is why many herbal remedies that are used don't work. Many people misuse herbs incorrectly and give up on herbal remedies. For me, this is akin to giving up on good health, even at minimal cost.

Sourcers of herbs can be complicated for anyone who is new to herbal medicine. I'm sure you are wondering what is the best method to source herbs. You don't need to know anything special in order to source high-quality herbs.

Contrary what Harry Potter and other fantasy novelists might have you believe, powerful herbs don't require you to travel to mystical places in order to get them. Making potions is not possible with herbs. They're scientifically proven to treat many conditions.

To fully harness the therapeutic benefits of herbal medicine, you just need to understand some key points, such as the best time to harvest, which plant parts to pick and many more details that we will discuss shortly.

Buying

Native American herbs are readily available due to their popularity. To obtain these herbs, you don't need to travel far to see the Native Americans, such as Arizona, California or Oklahoma. It might be worth searching locally for herbs in nearby stores. You shouldn't hesitate to purchase high quality herbs if you are sure they have them in stock.

If you're looking for native American herbs to buy from a local seller, there are several other factors to be aware of. These are:

* The quality of the soil used to grow them.

* The method of cultivation

* The process or drying of herbs;

* The seller's method of storage.

For Native American herbs and any other herb, the soil type is crucial. They could lose or reduce their medicinal properties if they were grown in unsuitable soil. It would only be junk to eat them and can even be dangerous for your health.

You can then find out about the cultivation practices and methods used in growing your herbs. Is the herb hydroponically or soil-based? What fertilizers did they use How did they manage pests (the use of chemicals)? You can ask them the following questions to verify their answers, no matter if you are buying from a modern producer or a local one.

You should also look at the way that the herbs were treated after harvest. This is where contamination can begin for most herbs. Most herbs would lose their medicinal properties if they have to go through high temperatures. The leaves' color will indicate this. If plants appear darker than they should, it is a sign that they are losing their quality.

It is also crucial to store your plants. How has the family stored their plants since they got them? This will tell you if they are going to sell them.

You should confirm with local producers the type of soil they use to grow their plants before you pay. Also, ask them for a test of the herbs to ensure they are clean and free from any contamination.

Cultivation

It is possible to grow your herbs yourself. There are many growing methods you can choose from and you can grow your own plants while saving money.

Whichever method you choose, be it hydroponic, soil-based or outdoor, the results will be the same. Make sure that your herbs have enough of the following items:

* Adequate lighting;

* Get enough water.

* If you have them growing in soil and indoors, you might consider composting to increase the quality of your soil.

You also need to keep your herbs free from rodents or other harmful pests. They can damage them over time.

Here are some tips and tricks to help you grow and harvest herbs at home.

* Get all the information you need about the plants before you begin to plant them. To care for a plant you need to be able understand it. This will allow you to provide the best possible care and yield.

Information on the best practices to use when growing any plant is also necessary. This includes information on which fertilizers you should use, which to avoid and how to manage your plants.

* Not only can you save money but it will also allow you to beautify the home. Native American herbs can be grown indoors to add vibrant color to your living space. This is where perennial plants such as echinacea excel.

* Make sure to tend to your plants often. Plant them right away. Plants are like pets and need to be looked after.

Wild-crafting

Some herbs are considered weeds. They can be extracted from their natural habitat from bushes, trees or any other place they may naturally occur. These wild-crafted herbs are as good as organically grown. They are better because they grow naturally, and don't have to be exposed to soil contamination or high temperatures, which could lead them to lose most of their beneficial ingredients. Dandelion, for instance, is more beneficial when it is wild grown. Their roots, leaves, flowers and roots have more medicinal value when you weed them than if they were bought or planted.

Some herbs, however, are endangered. It is recommended that you grow these herbs instead of going out into the wild to wild-craft them. You must follow these guidelines if wild crafting is something you are planning to do. These guidelines are important to remember:

Follow the abundance. Only harvest from the places where the kind of herb that you seek can be bought in bulk.

* Make sure that the herb that you plan to wild craft is not listed in the endangered or

threatened list. This will ensure that you are contributing to society and the general welfare of life.

* Use common sense when wild crafting. Don't overharvest any herb. Don't over-harvest any plants. Wild crafting is best when you only need a small amount of herbs.

* Do NOT fully harvest mature, seed-producing or flowering plants. Try to choose smaller plants to harvest.

Storing Herbs

Herbs are delicate creatures. They lose their medicinal properties gradually if left alone without being dried or processed. Drying herbs is the best way to keep their medicinal properties intact until you are ready to use them.

The best herbs retain their strength when kept in a cool, dark, and airtight area. Even more surprising is the fact that many sellers and producers keep their herbs in large containers to keep them out of oxygen (which can cause their strength to decrease), dust, and other external elements. They also protect them from weather conditions that can cause their properties to deteriorate over time, leading to eventual death.

Maintain an average temperature. The temperature at which herbs are exposed should not exceed 100 degrees Fahrenheit. If they do, the constituents of the herb will slowly disappear. It is harmful to the herbs' medicinal properties to expose them directly to light. You can store them in dark bottles and jars, glass containers, or plastic bags.

If you have leftover herbs you want to keep, the best way to do so is to shake them up, take the stems off the leaves, and then spread them out on a dark, clean surface. This allows your herbs to breathe, and it also makes it easier to spot and remove any potential pests.

You should dry herbs quickly if you want to preserve their power. The faster the plants lose power, the shorter the drying period. For the best results, keep the drying period between 5-7 day. They must be completely dried before they can be broken. This is because they can keep their constituents and property until you are ready to use them.

Tossing tree barks is a very simple process. This involves removing the bark from the tree to get rid of any polluted areas and any pests that might have settled there.

Roots might require you to wash them to remove all soil particles. Once they are clean, store them in large airtight container.

Conclusion

It doesn't matter what method you use to source herbs or how long you keep them, you should ensure you do it correctly for the particular plant type. There are many herbs that can be used, and not all will like to be stored or sourced the same way. It's important to get to know your plants before you go ahead and source or store them. Some plants are best when used as soon as possible after being sourced. Other plants will do well if stored.

It is important that you dry your plants before you put them in storage. They should be placed on a surface that is level so they have ventilation. After they dry, move them into your container. When they're in the jar make sure that the temperature is below 100°F. As I mentioned, plants that are exposed to heat tend to deteriorate much faster. If you plan to store them, make sure to avoid high temperatures. This will allow you to harness the healing power of their plants.

Chapter 3: Herbal Preparations

What is most important in herbal medicine? The way we extract the herbs and make them into consumables that are easy to absorb. Modern technology allows us to extract, filter, and distill herbs faster and more efficiently to create standard medicines that we can consume today.

But, these modernized methods for making herbal remedies aren't necessary. To get the best results from these herbal remedies, there are many simple preparation options. We take you back in time and show you some of these effective preparation methods used by the Native American.

This chapter will cover the basics of herbal preparation, how to properly use some remedies, common ingredients, and what you need to do to get them to work.

Methods and Processes

* Brew/Infusion; This method is commonly used when making herbal teas. It's as easy as pouring

boiling hot water over the herbs, fresh or dried. This water infuses leaves with the desired components and helps extract them from the plants. You can make this yourself by adding 2 tsps dried or fresh herbs to a cup. Then boil some water and pour the water into the cup. You can leave the cup to brew for some time before you start to take.

* Decoction is the process of boiling herbs in water to release the plant's healing properties. Decoction is used for all hard plants, including roots, tree barks, stems, and seeds.

Make a homemade remedy using this method. Put enough herbs in a small saucepan. Allow it to cool off and turn off the heat.

* Percolation - This is the same process we use to make our coffees. It involves grinding your herbs to dry them, then adding some water to moisten the herb. Finally, you leave it for around 12-24 hours. You can then drip water through the ground herbs mixture using a valve. Let the liquid run until it is in a sufficient amount.

* Tincture - This process is similar to percolation but involves soaking in alcohol or glycerin. This allows the active constituents of the plants to be extracted from the liquid. Tinctures typically contain several herbs to ensure high levels of active ingredients. This would require that you soak the herbs in any liquids or chemicals for up 2 weeks before straining the liquid and eating.

* Dual (Double-Extraction): Like tinctures, dual extraction requires alcohol.

Double extraction is very simple, even though its name may sound technical. It is as easy as:

* Fill a container and add your herbs.

* Pour some alcohol into the container to cover the herbs.

* Allow this mixture to rest for 2 weeks.

* Make sure to shake the active ingredients at least once a day while you wait.

*After speaking for a while, strain out the alcohol content and put aside. This is your first extraction.

* Allow the herbs to simmer in water for approximately 30 minutes. Allow the water to cool and drain it from your first extraction.

* Fomentation is required to prepare herbs using this process. Once you have sufficient preparation, dip your cotton in the alcohol content. Then you can apply it to the injured area. Applying too much of the preparation to your skin can cause irritation and even make it red.

* Poultice. Use the dried herbs you have to grind into a powder and place the ground herbs on the skin where you want it to be used.

* Powder: You don't need any liquid to make herbs powder. All you need is to dry them and grind them.

* Oils, creams lotions, and salves can be made with fresh or dried herb. To extract the oil, first heat the oil and then cook the herbs. You can thicken the oil by adding beeswax. Apply or use according to your preference. You can apply as much as your heart desires to your face and any other areas on your body.

Tools are required

Making your own herbs requires a few key tools. The majority of these tools are essential for making the best herbal remedies. You don't necessarily need to have a lot of tools. All you need is the following tools, which you may already have in your own kitchen.

* Pots

* Saucepan

* Kettle

* Mason jars

* Wire mesh strainers

* Cheesecloth

* Measure cups and spoons

* Bottles

* Labels

* Valve

* Blender

* Mortar & Pestle

* Cotton cloth

* Knife

* Scissors

Although these tools can make life easier, they're not required.

* French press

* Thermos

* Press pot

* Herb grinder/coffee maker

Common Ingredients in Herbal Preparations

For most herbal preparations, all you need is the herbs and water. You will need some other ingredients to get maximum benefit from the herbs you use and to make some herbal remedies more easy to apply. These ingredients include:

* Alcohol: Alcohol, a strong substance used to extract the hidden qualities of plants, is also known as "alcohol". This is why alcohol is commonly used to extract the constituents of herbs.

* Apple cider Vinegar: This is the preferred version of distilled white wine vinegar, if you plan to use your herbs infusions and/or directly on your skin.

* Honey: Unprocessed honey can also be used in herbal preservatives.

* Oils such as olive oil, almond or grapeseed oil and cocoa butter, shea oil, shea oil, lanolin, and tallow are great oils for making herbal remedies.

* Beeswax is required for oils and creams, lotions, and salves.

* Witch Hazel Extract: This ingredient is great for adding to herbal remedies, especially when used topically.

* Rose water, also known as rose water, is often used in skincare.

* Epsom salts, and sea salts: Salts are also known to enhance the healing properties in herbs.

* Gelatin capsules are: these can be used for making your own Native American herbal medications into capsules. Before swallowing, grind your herbs to a powder.

Methods of application

We have already spoken about the most common ways to process herbs. We'll briefly discuss the various application methods of Native American herbs in this section.

* Facial masks made with Native American herbs: Chamomile flow (elder ginger root), ginseng, ginkgo biloa, ginseng, and elder ginger root are some of the Native American herbs you can use to make your own facial masques. These herbs are well-known for their ability to remove excess oil, soften the skin, reduce pores, and complete heal the skin. To brighten

and smoothen your skin, you can combine several of these herbs.

* Hair Care and Skin Care: Native American herb extracts can also be used in oils, creams and lotions that you can use on your skin. Rose, milk thistle, and sage are all great anti-aging herbs that you can use to moisturize your skin and promote softness and smoothness.

Make your own shampoos using these herbs to cleanse your hair and remove any hair shaft residue left behind by modern haircare products. These herbs are better than chemical-based products that can damage hair over time. Native herbs are also quick to remedy dandruff, hair lice, and other hair issues.

* Poultices, Oils, Salves and Balms: I can make my own herbal poultices by grinding and lightly oiling herbs. Then, I can apply it to open wounds, painful joint areas, and any other affected areas using a cotton fabric or other "gentle".

Herbal oils are more affordable than processed ones. It'd be great if your herbs were soaked in olive or other oils mentioned in the previous section. This will extract the medicinal components of the herbs and allow them to be mixed with the oils for use as ointments, salves, etc.

* Baths - Instead of applying herbs to your skins in creams and lotions you can also make bathing so soaps.

Native American herbs, such as coneflower, calendula and echinacea are very effective in treating burns and rejuvenating the skin.

* Teas: Here is where the infusion process, which we mentioned earlier, comes in. It is possible to "infuse" herbs with medicinal properties and make delicious hot or cold teas. This is especially recommended for delicate plants which might lose their contents quickly due to heat or adding alcohol.

* Tinctures - Herbs can also contain alcohol, glycerin and vinegar. These herbs may be consumed hot or in a mixture with juice. They can taste a bit bitter, but they will easily be absorbed into your body.

* Scents & Fragrances. Some native herbs can also serve as body fragrances. They can even be used for treating your environment. The way you smell can affect the way people see you. If you and your surroundings don't have a great odor, it will be hard for people around you to feel comfortable with you.

Fragrances are often expensive and can be disconcerting. But what we don't realize is that there are herbs in nature that can make us smell better. These are the three most commonly used herbs: pow pow (sweetgrass), sage and sweetgrass. They can be used for any occasion, and they are also popular with perfumers.

Caution

Many people believe herbal medicines can be overused because they have no side effects and are considered "natural". No, herbal remedies can't be used excessively. Side effects of herbal medicines are similar to modern drugs. They can be triggered by overdose, incorrect use, or misinterpretation. You should consult a doctor or herbalist to determine the best dosages for you and the possible side effects that may occur if you take them incorrectly. A high dose of raw elderberries may cause serious reactions. St. John's wort is another herb that, according to research can cause side effects when taken with antidepressants.

Research has also revealed that some herbs can be very dangerous for mothers who are pregnant or nursing. These herbs should be avoided to ensure their safety.

You should ensure that you are using the right herbs before you can use them. Here are some safety guidelines to help you make best use of herbal remedies you will be learning how to make in Native American Herbalism.

* Native American herbs should be avoided by pregnant women and nursing mothers. American Ginseng (or rosemary) has been reported to increase hormone levels in some individuals and cause uterus cramps in others.

* Children under the age of 2 should not be given alcohol-based herbal products to their livers. This can cause serious health problems.

* Some herbs are not allowed to be taken with other drugs. Talk to a professional herbalist if your other medications are being used in conjunction with herbs. Ginkgo biloba and Licorice root herbs, as well as St. John's wort, should not be taken with heart disease medications. To determine if any herbal remedy is safe for you, it is important to consult your doctor.

For those with asthma or epilepsy, avoid St. John's wort and other herbal remedies. The herbs can be harmful to patients with epilepsy and may cause seizures.

* Only buy herbs from licensed shops to make sure they aren't contaminated and that they don't lose their healing properties. Make sure the labels and safety information are clearly visible on all products you purchase. Be sure to check the labels on all packages. Make sure to only purchase herbs in darkened packages. Avoid herbal manufacturers who don't offer sufficient evidence or information about product quality. You should only buy herbs that

have been approved by U.S. Pharmacopeia and NSF International if you're located in the US.

Summary

In this chapter we have discussed the various herbal methods for preparation, application, as well safety tips. Next, we will discuss the herbs themselves. What are the Native American herbs? And how can they be used to treat ailments? Let's start the next chapter together.

Chapter 4: Native American Medicinal Plants

You may have guessed by the title that we would be briefly reviewing some Native American medicinal plants. There are over 100 Native American herbs. We won't be able to go through them all here. We'll still try to include as many as possible the most common ones we can find.

Many people don't know that there are alternative herbal medicines to modern medicine. We can use them for almost all types of illnesses. Many would like to believe that herbal medicine (i.e. Research has not been able to support this belief. But, contrary to popular belief, there is growing evidence that herbs have powerful healing properties. Modern medicine did not begin until the 18thcentury, when the Industrial Revolution took place. Humans relied heavily on herbal medicine before the Industrial Revolution. Let's think about this...

Agave Americana: This is the juice from the American agave plant. It's used in the production of agave syrup, which is a sweetener to replace sugar or honey in foods and drinks. This plant improves body metabolism, strengthens heart health and helps with depression. Agave, which is safe for pregnant mothers, is also one of its most useful properties. It improves their health as well as that of their baby.

Alder bark (alnus). It is used in the treatment of bleeding gums, throat inflammation, throat pain, and throat pain. It is also used in the preparation of lotions and poultices that treat all kinds of skin conditions including burns, infected wounds, eczema, and hemorhoids. Native American folktales prove that alder is also an effective aphrodisiac.

Aloe barbadensis (aloe barbadensis), like many Native American herbs, can be used to treat a variety medical conditions. It soothes pain, heals cuts, improves digestion systems, promotes good oral health, clears skin and smoothens it. Do you want more sexual energy? Aloe vera gel can improve your sexual performance and your libido.

Amaranth (amaranthus.sp. Amaranth (amaranthus.sp.): Native Americans generously gave amaranth to us. It is one of nature's most nutritious and common herbal grains. This plant is rich with fiber, antioxidants and micronutrients. This herb is often used to help with weight loss, inflammation, and reduce cholesterol.

Angelica (angelica Atropurpurea). This is a common plant in Arkansas, USA. The natives often mix it with tobacco to smoke. Angelica is the ideal herb to use if your symptoms include a cold, menopause, arthritis, or other ailments. It can also be used to treat respiratory problems and cancer.

Viburnum Dentatum: Arrow wood is great for treating cramps, and inducing vomiting.

Wild Anise or Myrrhis Ornamenta (Myrrhis odorata),: All parts of this amazing plant are useful. This plant can treat a runny nose, cough, intestinal problems, and other symptoms such as runny or irritable bowel syndrome. It can also be used to stimulate appetite and diuretic effects.

Balsam Fir or abies balsamea is a common remedy for external wounds. It can also be used to treat colds and sore throats.

Barberry (berberis species): Barberry can be used to remove kidney stones and relieve kidney pain.

Bearberry (Arctostaphylos. uva–ursi) is an exceptional Native American plant. It's what you could call "small yet powerful." Bearberry is a low growth plant that also has powerful therapeutic powers, as the name implies. It can be used to treat inflammation of the urinary tract and bacteria in menstrual problems. It also works well as an anti-inflammatory.

Black Gum Bark (nyssa, sylvatica),: Instant relief of chest pains.

Bloodroot (sanguinariacanadensis), a juice that is extracted from the plant, can be used to treat fever, respiratory issues, sore throats.

Candle Bush (cassia lata),: This plant can be used for fungal infections. This can be used on the body and skin. They can also be used for treating symptoms like fever, stomach ulcers, syphilis as well as snake bites.

Cascara Sagrada or Buckthorn: Botanically known by rhamnus purshiana. This natural laxative has been used for thousands upon thousands of years.

Native Americans used catnip, or Napeta Cataria, to treat symptoms such as hives. Today, it is used for much more. Catnip can even be infused and used to treat anxiety, nervousness as well as conditions like insomnia or digestive problems. The plant is also used to treat digestive upsets such as gassing and indigestion. Catnip, along with many Native American plants is a diuretic. This plant can be used in a variety of ways to improve urination, decrease water retention, or treat similar conditions.

Typha latifolia (cattail): If your knowledge of herbal medicine is extensive, chances are you have heard the name "cattail." It's one of the most well-known Native American plants, and it is used in food as well as in herbal medicines. Cattail can be used to aid digestion, soothe the stomach, heal toothaches and prevent cancer. They can also be used to treat skin infections and provide antiseptic properties.

Devil's claw: (harpagophytum). Although this name may seem threatening, Devil's Claw's not dangerous. You'll be surprised at how versatile this Native American herb can be. Native Americans have used Devil's Claw for centuries to treat various ailments, from fever to indigestion to arthritis to skin conditions. This tea can be used to treat diabetes, gout or back pain as well as to reduce swelling and joint diseases.

Dogwood (cornus Florida): The bark from this tree is used for treating various conditions, including colic, cold and fever.

Elderberry (sambucus cadensis) can be used for treating a variety of medical conditions such as headaches, indigestion and cold.

Geranium (geranium sp. Geranium (geranium, sp.

Ginseng (panax.ginseng), another powerful plant, was gifted to us from the Native

Americans. It is used to treat cramps headaches, asthma and emphysema, as well as for menstrual problems and stroke.

Golden Alexander (Zizia Aurea: The roots, stem, leaves and root can all be used to treat inflammation, sores as well as menstrual problems, vitiligo, psoriasis and other conditions.

Healall (Prunella vulgaris): Was regarded by the ancients as the "holy herb" God sent to cure all of our illnesses. Healall isn't able to cure all diseases. However it can be used for treating many conditions including fatigue, fever, stomach problems, heart disease, internal bleeding, sore throat, sore throat, liver, and other weaknesses. It has been proven to be a valuable agent in research for serious diseases like cancer, AIDS or diabetes.

Honeysuckle or lonicera: Has many healing properties. It can be used for hepatitis treatment, asthma, arthritis. mumps. rheumatoid. pneumonia.

Wild American Licorice: Glycyrhiza Lepidota (glycyrrhiza licorice): The refreshing effects of the licorice root are well-known and have long been used in food, drinks, and candies. It is used by herbalists to treat conditions such as stomach upset, fatigue, food poisoning, and even bronchitis.

Chimaphilaumbellata (Pipsissewa): This plant is commonly used as a "blood purifier" and can be used to treat gonorrhoea.

Evening Primrose, also known as EPO, comes from plant seeds. It was used historically to treat sore throat, digestive disorders and bruises. But its use has expanded over the years to include skin issues such as acne and eczema. EPO can be used to treat skin problems, such as acne, hot flashes and bone pain.

Red Clover (Trifolium Pratense) : This plant has been used throughout the years to treat inflammation and respiratory ailments. Red clover can also be used to treat heart conditions. This is done by decreasing cholesterol and improving blood flow.

Saw Palmetto: This herb (serenoa.repens), is commonly used for food. However, it has been long used as an herbal remedy for indigestion. It is also known to increase appetite.

Greek Valerian (polemonium Reptans: This was used by the aboriginals to induce vomiting, excessive skin sweating, and epidermis inflammation.

White Hellebore, veratrumviride: This is used mainly to treat external injuries and pain.

Willow (salix.sp.): This tree's bark as well as its leaves can be used for pain relief and aches.

Wild Rose (Rosa), although it may sound gentle on your tongue, this rose has powerful properties that can eliminate certain diseases. Native Americans use Wild Roses to treat sore throats and common colds. Wild rose tea can also help with hypertension, kidney problems, and stimulating your bladder.

Yarrow, also known as Achillea millefolium, was used by Native Americans for excessive bleeding. Poultices are made from yarrow and used topically on open wounds to help with blood clotting. Yarrow has been used to heal stomach problems, improve digestion and enhance the function of the intestines.

Yucca (yucca fibrosa), is one of the most common plants Native Americans use to make their foods. It is used for treating diabetes, Colitis (migraines), colitis and hypertension.

HERBALISM

What Is Herbalism, and What Does It Signify?

Herbalism can be described as a form herbalism that uses herbs, plants, extracts, and other natural remedies to treat various diseases. Native American Shamans used their knowledge about herbs and plants as a source of healing medicines. Shamanic Healing is Native American medicine which combines herbal medicine and the guidance of the spirit world to treat the whole person.

Herbalism and Herbalists

Native American healers and herbalists had a wide range of principles that combined spiritual and bodily healing. Native American healers considered plants and trees, as well as flowers and herbs, to possess wisdom and spirit. The Shaman will only harvest what is needed to make Herbalism work. Ritual rituals and prayers, poems and chants were used to aid in the healing of herbs.

Native American Herbalism & Remedies

Native American Herbalism involved the use of various herbs and plants indigenous to North America. A detailed list of Native American Herbalism's herbal remedies and medicines can be found in the A-Z Chart of Natural Herbal Herbs or our post on Herbal Remedies. Native Americans were able heal, cleanse, and purify the bodies of their loved ones using herbal medicine. Herbalism's natural Plants & Medicinal Herbs were used by the Shaman to normalize and regulate bodily functions. The abundance of vitamins and minerals found in herbs is impressive. Herbalism methods have the added advantage that they increase energy levels. This allows the body and immune system to heal themselves. Herbalism relies on herbs and Medicinal Herbs, which are natural remedies and natural medicine that Native Americans used to live off of the natural products provided by nature.

Native American Herbalism: Natural Treatments

Native American Herbalism was a collection of over 20,000 North American plants. Only 2000 were used to treat ailments. The Shaman needed to have a good understanding of the herbs' medicinal properties, how to gather them, what parts to use and how to prepare them for treating tribe members. The Shaman was believed to have abilities or powers that enabled him use Herbalism to a degree that was not apparent to the average person. The Native American Herbalism that the Shaman used could cure, heal and influence people's souls or spirits.

Herbal Medicine's Disadvantages and Advantages

Herbal medicine

* There is no incurable illness, but a lack of willpower.

* There are no unutilized herbs.

Herbal medicines, also known by plant materials, Herbalism, can be used to treat ailments and accidents with whole plants or parts. Herbal medicine is used in medicine to treat or prevent disease and disorders. It also promotes well-being, healing, and overall health. A variety of medicines and formulations can be made from herbs. Herbal medicines are considered the most ancient form of healthcare.

A wide range of ailments can be treated with herbal products, including depression, the common cold, and the flu. The World Health Organization (WHO), defines specific herbal drugs as complete, brand-named medicinal products that contain active ingredients and secretive sections or other plant material. The World Health Organization has set out specific criteria for assessing herbal medicines' effectiveness, safety, and consistency.

The World Health Organization reports that herbal medicines are used for significant health care by 80 per cent of the global population.

Some countries also allow herbs to be covered with organic or conventional active constituents. Ayurvedic medicine, Naturopathic and Homeopathic medicines all include herbs. Herbs are generally healthy because they come from nature. The popularity of herbal drugs has increased dramatically due to side effects and toxicity of allopathic medications. The popularity of herbal products has increased over the past several decades among non-prescription users.

Herbal Medicines have many benefits.

* Cost-Effectiveness

* High Potency And Efficacy

* Enhanced tolerance

* More Security

* There are less side effects

* Accessibility Available for All

* Recyclable Materials

Herbal Drugs Have Their Advantages

* Not being capable of treating injuries and illnesses that develop quickly

* Self-medicating is risky.

* Standardizations contain a lot of complexity.

HOW TO RECOGNIZE HERBS.

How to Recognize the Different Herbs in Your Garden

It is simple to get familiar with the herb's leaf characteristics. To help you identify the different herbs, look at their sizes, colors, and heights. Once you learn to associate certain aromas with spices, then you will be able identify them by their smell.

Identification by Characteristics

Watch how the herbs grow to discover more about them. Even though rosemary can become a big bush, oregano will stay close to the ground while sage and sage may spread out. Basil and Thyme will look more natural in the new form they have, while Parsley will still be visible as a garnish. Sage and oregano both have furry leaves. Basil and thyme, on the other hand, have smooth leaves.

Aromatic Recognition

If you're familiar with the aroma of a specific herb you can still use your nose to determine if there is any part of the plant that you need to achieve the full scent. Dill is a familiar smell. If you are familiar with their names, you will still recognize rosemary, oregano (sage), and thyme.

It is essential to recognize herbs from a garden.

Herbs to Grow

An herb is a plant that doesn't have a woody root and returns to its perennial roots each winter. A herb is a plant that provides significant seasonings for food preparation in the garden. You can use herbs to create fragrances for cosmetics and medicinal purposes. Some herbs can be woody, which is contrary to the herbaceous concept.

American pioneers used herbs to season their food. They were also used to treat illnesses, store linens on floors, cover the unfavorable taste of meats prior to refrigeration, as home dye fabrics, and for fragrances.

When a wider range of dried herbs were made available in supermarkets, gardening herbs in the gardens fell out favor. Due to the growing popularity of ethnic foods and the recognition that fresh herbs have distinct flavors, more gardeners are planting at least a few herbs for future use, drying, or freezing. As interest in herbal medicine grows, herb growing has become more common. Some herbs are decorative.

General Cullture

SunLight

While most herbs can be grown easily, it is essential to pick the right place. Only a few plants such as sweet cicely, angelica and woodruff can thrive in partial shade. Plants that get six to 8 hours of direct sunshine per day will produce the most oils that give the herbs their flavor. Even though many herbs can tolerate light shade, they will still grow and thrive in a sunny area.

The Soil

All soils are suitable for herb growth. It should not be acidic, nor alkaline. A pH range between 6.5 and 7.0 is best for spice growth.

Organic matter is essential for herb growth. Most herbs don't need much nutrition in their soil. In highly productive soils, excessive foliage can lead to a lack of flavor.

You can incorporate 4 inches of compost, peat moss, or compost in your garden while you prepare average soils to improve soil condition. This will help preserve moisture.

Drainage.

When choosing a place for a herb garden, drainage is essential. While most essential herbs do not grow well in wet soils (except for mint, angelica, or lovage), a few of them do.

If you have no access to the land, you'll need the site to be changed. Raised beds or underground drainage tiles are essential for successful herb growing.

Preparation

Once you have decided on a spot, plant the soil to a depth between 12 and 18 inches. After that, level it. If only a thin layer remains of topsoil on top of the gravelly soil, remove it temporarily. Add organic matter to the soil to break it down. After the subsoil is improved, you can replace it. Even if your topsoil quality is higher than your subsoil, you still need organic matter.

Pest

Herbs are not often attacked by pests or diseases. Some areas are infected with rust. Some herbs may be affected by spider mites during hot, dry weather.

Aphids attack anise, caraway (dill), fennel, and dill. If the conditions are right, grasshoppers as well as certain caterpillars can infest herbs. The problem usually does not arise until control is necessary. Pesticides must be labeled to identify food crops, if they are being used for culinary purposes.

Seeds For Propagation

You can grow many herbs from seeds. You can plant seeds indoors in the late winter using either flats or pots. The best conditions for their development are a sunny window and low temperatures (60 degrees F). As you would with pepper plants or salvia, young garden plants need to be treated in the same manner as other plants.

Start smaller seeds in February. After the danger of frost has passed you can transplant them into individual containers and place them in the greenhouse. For best results, seeds should be sown lower than usual.

Some herbs are more difficult to transplant. In the greenhouse, sow them directly. Don't transplant anise coriander dill or fennel. Instead, plant them immediately in the park.

Direct seeding should be done in spring after the dangers of frost have passed, and the soil has started to warm up. A good, level seedbed should be made from the soil. As a general rule, seed should be sown at twice the depth of the original seeds.

Cuttings Propagation and Division

Some herbs may be multiplied asexually by cutting, dividing or layering.

Many perennials come with flexible branches which are perfect for layering. All profit is made by the division of tarragon, mint, and even chives. It is possible to use cuttings for lavender, lemon balms, scentedgeraniums and rosemary cultivation.

Safe, well-established plants can be used to take herb cuttings at any time in the late spring or summer. Cuttings taken in fall will take longer for them to root than spring cuttings. Healthy tip growth is the best source of cuttings. Not recommended: Cuttings from weak stems or old, hardened woody stems.

You can make a 3-4 inch-long cut by cutting just below the nodes. Most herbs can root in 2 to 4 weeks. After they are rooted, keep them in the pots in a sunny place or in a coldframe. In the following season, you can plant them in an outside permanent spot.

Two to four year old mature plants are good candidates for division. For plants like French tarragons, mints and chives, division allows for a slight uptake. Before the development of herbs begins, divide them in spring. After digging up the plant, cut it into pieces. Replant the area and keep it moist until they have the chance to grow.

Layering perennial herbs like rosemary, wintersavory, lemon balm and winter savory is the most efficient and reliable way to increase their numbers. The idea is to attach roots to a stem and allow them to grow. After rooting a stem, remove the new plant. Pick a branch that is close to ground level and can bend towards the soil. The stem should be bent vertically from the top six to ten inches. Scrape any bark that is left behind at the bend. Keep the bent section of the branch 3 to 6 inches below ground. Attach a wire loop to secure it. To hold it upright, you can place a small stake at the top. Wet thoroughly the area.

You can layer any time from spring through the late summer. Let the rooted shoot remain in place until next spring. You can then remove it from the parent plants and place it anywhere you like.

Winter Protection

Many herbs are vulnerable to winter harm. Therefore, winter protection is highly recommended for perennial herbs. Many herbs have roots that are shallow and can grow out of the soil in spring, when it thaws. For sufficient coverage, you can spread a layer of 4-inch-deep mulch over the seeds. Mulch can either be made with evergreen boughs and grass or from oak leaves. Mulch is made after the ground freezes in the winter months. Only remove mulch as soon as new growth begins to appear in the early spring. Fluff the mulch up in the spring if it becomes compacted during winter snowfall.

How to Keep Fresh Herbs Well

The easiest way to keep herbs fresh is to pick them right from the field. Some people don't have the green thumb necessary to plant herbs outdoors. Yes, you can have an indoor herb garden. However, there isn't enough space in my home so it would be impossible to grow herbs right now. So, I thought this would be a great time to share my method for keeping fresh herbs safe. This is a great way to keep fresh herbs in your home, as well as store-bought spices.

Tender Vs. Abrasive

You must first determine whether the herb is still tender or stiff in order to know how to properly store it. Basil, parsley, and citro are examples of delicate herbs, with soft stems. A woody stem is a characteristic feature of thymy plants such as rosemary and marjoram.

Herbs to Be Washed

Some people claim that washing herbs adds moisture. But, in reality, herbs are already wet when they come home from the store. My experience shows that herbs thrive when they are rinsed under cold running water and spinned in a salad spinning machine. By washing them and turning them, you can get rid of any bacteria or other debris that could lead to decay. This is especially true of herbs with tender leaf. Use a salad spinner if you don't have one. Wait until the spices are ready for use before washing.

How to keep them fresh

Tender herbs: Basil, Cilantro, Parsley

After the herbs were washed, trim the stems. All leaves that have turned brown or become wilted should be removed. Add 12 inch of water in a Mason or glass jar. Arrange the herbs as a bouquet in the pot. You can store parsley and cilantro by covering them loosely with a resealable zip-lock bag or cling film. Cover the spices by using the lid of either a large Mason-jar or quart saucepan. Refrigerate any leftovers. This works well with dill, mint, and even tarragon. To store basil, let it dry out and then place it on a counter to catch some light. Refill the water as needed or if it begins discoloring.

Hard Herbs - Rosemary (thyme), oregano, marjoram, and oregano

On a damp towel, arrange the herbs in a single line. Roll the herbs and wrap them in plastic wrap or plastic bags. Refrigerate any leftovers. This method is also good with sage, salty, and chives.

How long will it last?

When properly cared for fresh herbs can survive for up to 3 weeks. Below are some of the most well-known herbs, along with their average livespan. When spices start to become darkened and brittle or if the stems are showing signs of mold, it's time to toss them.

Tender herbs

* Parsley for 3 weeks

* Dill 3 weeks

* Cilantro - 3 weeks

* Mint- 2 weeks

* Tarragon-- 3 Weeks

* Basil - 2 weeks

Hard Herbs

* Rosemary- 3 weeks

* Oregano - 2 weeks

* Thyme 2 weeks

* Sage - 2 weeks

* Savory for 2 weeks

* Chives for 1 Week

13 Types of Fresh herbs

1. Cilantro

Chinese parsley leaf, Chinese parsley koyendoro Mexican parsley, and pak chee green coriander coriander coriander green, dhania green coriander coriander, green coriander.

Characteristics of cilantro: You either love it or hate it. Some describe cilantro's flavour as bright and citrusy, while others describe it as soapy. This herb is found in Vietnamese, Mexican, Thai, and Indian dishes. Coriander is the name of the plant seeds that are used in pickling and boerewors. This South African sausage is also known as coriander.

What does cilantro look like? It has flat-leaf parsley like leaves, but it has narrower leaves with a lankier stalk.

2. Peppermint

Two of the most popular types of mint are peppermint or spearmint. The high concentrations of menthol found in peppermint have a strong, cooling aftertaste. On the other hand, spearmint tastes lighter and sweeter. If used in large quantities, curly and apple mints, as well as ginger and apple mints, impart the same flavor. Thai cuisines are dominated by mint, such as rolls, Middle Eastern food like tabbouleh and North African teas. Mint is often eaten with lamb and chocolate. Mint can also be used in sauces, jellies, and cocktails like the Mint Julep, Mojito, and other mint-based drinks.

What is the appearance and function of mint? All mints and spearmint have rough-fuzzy green leaves.

3. Parsley chopped

Some other names for this herb include flat-leafed Parsley (Italian), curly parsley and flat-leafed Parsley.

Characteristics Bouquet grin is used in French or Italian cuisine to spice different stocks, stews and soups. Flat parsley, however, has a spicy flavor while curly is more bland. There are also textural variations to them, as their names would suggest. Parsley cut into small pieces is added to many pastas and eggs. Its delicate flavor cuts through heavy creaminess while acting as a palate cleanser. You can make pesto by substituting basil for parsley to get a different flavor.

What is the appearance like of parsley leaves? Italian parsley has long, green, serrated leaves. Curly parsley has twisted leaves, which are also green as their name suggests.

4. Dill

Some other names for this herb include dillweed, dill-leaf, and dill weed.

Dill is a powerful herb that evokes strong reactions in people. Some like it for its freshness and greenness, while others dislike it due to its earthy flavor. It is commonly associated with Scandinavian cuisine and salmon, but it can also be found on other continents such as Greece (tzatziki), India (corn) and Russia (borscht) (Eastern Europe). Dill is commonly used in pickling and pairs well with potatoes or dips made using mayonnaise/sour cream.

What is the appearance like of dill? This herb looks more like a delicate, intricate fern with soft leaf that resembles superfine hairs.

5. Basil

Other names for this plant are sweet basil, purple basil, Thai basil, and Genovese basil.

Basil is America's most used herb. Italian basil has a peppery flavor and mild anise flavour. It tastes sweeter that purple basil. You can use sweet green basil in both Southeast Asia (green bird curry) or Italy (basil Pesto). Its dark color makes purple basil a wonderful garnish for dishes. Each of these leaves should always be added towards the end of cooking to get the best flavor. Thai basil is more aromatic and can withstand high heat.

What is the appearance or basil? Purple basil leaves tend to be smaller than sweet green leaves. Thai basil is characterized by its long leaves, which resemble mint and can range in color from green or purple to purple. In most cases, the stems are purple.

6. Oregano.

Marjoram is also known as wild marjoram and pot marijoram.

Oregano is a warm herb that adds warmth to dishes with its sweet and spicy flavor. Fresh oregano can sometimes be hard to find. Dryed oregano has an unpleasant taste so it is best to use sparingly. Mediterranean (Greek) Oregano is milder that Mexican oregano. This is why it is more commonly used for pizza seasonings. However, chili recipes sometimes use the latter.

What is the appearance like of oregano's leaves? Oregano leaves are flat and oval with varying textures. This herb can be mistaken for marjoram because it is of the same plant family.

The main difference is in the flavor. Oregano tends to be spicy, while marjoram has a lemony sweetness.

7. Rosemary's:

Rosemary's pine-like aroma and taste is strong. Tuscan classics such as schiacciata are made from flatbreads with rosemary-infused oils, chicken cacciatore, and rosemary. The Mediterranean region's rosemary is now a popular ingredient in Italian cuisine. It is delicious with chicken, pork, and even fish (especially when grilled). Vegetarians will enjoy potatoes that have been seasoning. Try rosemary shortbread cookies, a sweet-savory treat that's unique.

How does rosemary appear? Rosemary can have a distinctive appearance. It is formed as needles on woody stems. Cooking can be done with both branches and paws. (The stems can also be used to flavor soups, roasts, and other dishes).

8. Chives

Characteristics of Chives: Chives deep-green hollow stems have an oniony flavour that cuts through the richness found in foods like blue cheese, chive dressing, and even risotto cake. Finely chopped chives can be used to garnish.

What does it look like to have chives? This herb is related to onions, and other bulb veggies.

9. Sage

Characteristics of Sage include mild to intensely peppery flavors with hints and mint. Mixing sage with thick, rich and creamy foods such as meats, cheeses, creams, or sweet breads like cornbread, is a smart way to include it. Unlike delicate herbs, you can add the Sage early in your cooking process.

What is the appearance like of sage? Sage has light gray-green leaves with smooth, fluffy leaves.

10. Savory

Mountain savory is another name given to bean herb.

These are the two types savory. Summer savory tends to have a more peppery taste, while summer savory is more aromatic. This herb has been used in European cuisines long enough to be used in dishes like beans and pork. It can also be found in soups or stews with poultry and meat as well as beans.

What does it imply to be savory? It has narrow, narrow green leaves, which grow on long, thin stalks.

11. Thyme

Thyme's tiny, delicate leaves can be used in combination with other herbs or spices such as basil, lavender, and sage. Thyme is a vital component of the French seasoning herbs, herbes de Provence. It is also an essential ingredient in bouquet grin, a delicious blend of French herbs used for soups and stews. It's important in Middle Eastern cuisine, and it's also a key ingredient in za'atar. This herb mixture is often used to spice roasted meat, poultry, flatbreads like pita. For recipes, the leaves must be separated from their woody stems. The full herb will give it a more powerful aroma and taste.

What is the appearance and function of thyme It is not clear. Three types of thyme exist: English, German and French. German thyme is round with green stems; English thyme is pointed and has red-tinted leaves.

12. Tarragon

Some other names for this herb include Dragon herb.

Tarragon has a subtle anise flavor, similar to licorice/fennel. This is sweeter and less solid. You can often enjoy the herb with eggs, chicken, scallops, or eggs. Tarragon was once considered to be the king among herbs in French cuisine. It is not recommended to keep it for very long, so you should store it in a bottle with vinegar.

What is the appearance of Tarragon? Tarragon leaf appearance is shiny, slender and tapered. This herb makes a great garnish.

13. Marjoram

Some other names for this herb are sweet marjoram or knotted marjoram.

Marjoram has a lemony, grassy flavour that almost tastes sweet. Marjoram, similar to thyme is a great pairing for meats and poultry. Mixing marjoram, oregano and thyme in Mexico creates a vibrant pungent hierbas de colour similar to the French bouquet grin. Marjoram is used in tomato sauces as well white bean salads, fish dishes, vinaigrettes and other foods.

What is marjoram like? Marjoram looks like oregano because it has flat, round, green leaves. Both belong to the mint tribe. They share a common trait: their taste. Oregano has a spicy flavor, and marjoram is a soft one.

Tips for using Fresh Herbs

When cooking with herbs, you need to be cautious. Too much salt can cause other flavors to become overpowering. You will end up with bland dishes if you use too many salts (or not enough). Begin with a small amount. Gradually increase it until the desired level. These suggestions can help.

1. Look For Tall Herbs.

Select erect herbs that can stand upright without falling or becoming sloppy. You want brightly-colored leaves that are free from brown spots and with a fresh, clean scent.

2. Keep the herbs refrigerated.

You can keep herbs refrigerated to extend their shelf life. Small stems and leaves can be wrapped in a damp tissue and put in a plastic bag. Before refrigerating basil or other large quantities of herbs, make sure to stand them up in a glass that is filled with water.

3. Retire Fresh Herbs at the End

Use fresh herbs in recipes to preserve their flavor.

4. Dried Herbs in a Pinch

It is best to use fresh herbs and not dried. If you do have to use dried herbs one teaspoon for one tablespoon chopped mint would be a good rule.

5. Get involved in growing your own garden!

Consider growing herbs if space is available. There is no need for you to use all the herbs immediately so having fresh herbs in your arsenal reduces waste. Your local nursery garden will have seeds and seedlings. Some of the rarer varieties can be found at online catalog companies like Burpee, Park Seed and Park Seed.

When do you collect herb seeds?

How do I collect seeds? By placing the bucket on the ground, and bending the seed heads to the bucket. To prevent the roots from falling out, charges must be higher than the bucket when tipping. Some seed heads need to be crushed and some must be rolled in the hands. You can simply do this over the bucket to make sure everything fits together. Annuals are one of the easiest to grow from seed. However, you can also plant perennials, bulbs and other plants. F1 hybrids are special varieties that are developed for consistency and strength. Seedlings from these plants may have some variation. However, there are many benefits to this operation, which adds to its excitement!

It isn't always obvious when the seeds will be ready. It's possible for seeds to be harvested at a different time than when they're ready to be eaten. Some sources can be grown easily and should be stored until sowing, either under cover or outside. However, some sources are more difficult to germinate and may need special treatment like exposure to specific temperatures or soaking the seeds. When the seed heads and seeds are ready to be collected they tend to dry out, becoming straw-pale or papery. For next year's crop of seeds, you will want them to 'rocket or run to seed' if you wish to keep a few. The majority of seed selection is common sense. You can replicate what happens in nature when seeds mature by looking at the data.

How to get herb seeds

Choose A Day With No Wind and Sunny. Choose a healthy plant without any pests or diseases.

Seedpods that seem to be breaking should be avoided. Remove the entire seedhead.

Do not close the bag and crush the seed head. Invert the entire seed head upside down into the bag to mark it. The seeds will ripen in a cool, dry place.

Follow the Development of The Seeds. After the seedpods have opened, place the contents on a dry surface.

Extracted seeds must first be washed thoroughly before being stored. The best way to separate dried seeds from their chaff is to shake them through a series or graded sieves/screens. Put the seeds in the sieves. The largest mesh size is at the top, the smallest at its bottom. Give it a shake. One of the sieves is the best size to collect most sources. The other sieves are for scrap.

Clean the seed and place in a small sealed envelope. Keep the seed dry and in an open place until use. These seeds will last up to six years if they are kept in an airtight jar.

LIST AMERICAN NATIVE HERBS

Many herbs are available in different forms: capsules or powders, pills, capsules, teas or extracts, fresh and dried plants, as well as powders and tablets. Although many of these supplements are extremely beneficial, you should exercise caution when using them. Some of these can be dangerous for your health, especially if they are used in combination with other medications. If you are pregnant or nursing, consult your doctor before using herbal supplements.

Alfalfa

This is a species of flowering pea plant, which is formally known under the name Medicago Sativa. It has been used for centuries in herbal medicine and is now grown all around the globe. Vitamins B, which include vitamin C, vitamin D, and vitamin E, are high in vitamin, calcium, and other nutrients. They are well-known for treating digestive problems. Native Americans used it as a treatment for jaundice and to promote blood clotting. Alfalfa can now be used to treat arthritis, muscle pains, toxin elimination as well as bladder and kidney problems and symptoms such menopause. Alfalfa is known to worsen auto-immune conditions.

Ginseng From The United States

Panax Quinquefolius, also known as this plant, is part of the ivy famile and is native in eastern North America's hardwood forest. Native Americans used it for many purposes. It was used as a traditional medicine for colds and sinus problems, pneumonia, swelling reduction, and laxatives. The Seminoles, Seminoles, and Iroquois all smoked the herb as tobacco. It was dried for medicinal purposes by the Cherokee, Creek, Houma., Mimic and Mohegan. Some tribes used it to massage their bodies. One unusual way to use the herb was to attract a friend. Meskwaki woman used Ginsing to find a partner. Pawnee men used Ginsing for love charms. Europeans quickly recognized the benefits of the herb in the early 1700s. French traders in Quebec had already negotiated with Indians for any ginseng available. This effectively exterminated the herb's native habitats around Montreal.

Allspice

This spice is used to make many different dishes. Pimenta Dioica (also known as Pimenta) is a fragrant spice that can be used in cooking, seasoning, and as an herbal remedy. It is also known as Pimenta, Clove Pepper (New Spice), Kurundu, Myrtle Pepper (Jamaica Pepper), Pimenta, Clove Pepper, Clove Pepper, Clove Pepper, and Kurundu. Eugenol, a chemical ingredient in the oil that aids digestion, and is a pain reliever, is responsible for its healing properties. You can treat many conditions with dried unripe fruits in teas. The berries were also crushed and used in poultices or salves to treat sore joint pains, aching muscles, and other ailments.

Glycyrrhiza Lepidota

Wild licorice also known as wild garlic, is a native of North America. Its range extends from central Canada all the way to California, Texas, Virginia, and the southeastern United States. Its roots are used to treat colds, diarrhea, chest pain, fever, stomachaches, and hastening the placenta's delivery during childbirth by Native American tribes. It can also be used in a poultice, or swelling wash. The chewed root can be used as a sore throat remedy and toothache treatment. The mashed leaves are used as a poultice to treat sores.

Phoradendron Leucarpum

American Mistletoe, also known as American Mistletoe. Eastern Mistletoe, Hairy Mistletoe, Oak Mistletoe, Pacific Mistletoe, or Western Mistletoe are common. Europe's Druids used another mistletoe variety to treat convulsions. Native Americans used Phoradendron for blood pressure, respiratory disorder, seizures, headaches and contraception. The Cherokee made a tea that was used to cure headaches. While the Creek created a mixture to treat tuberculosis and other lung conditions. The root was commonly used by the Mendocino Indians in order to discourage pregnancy and prevent abortions. Other uses include chewing the root for toothaches and using a leaf decoction to sore limbs or joints. Some tribes also used the plant in religious rituals. You should use caution as the plant can be toxic.

Antelope Sage

James' Buckwheat can be described as a wild variety of buckwheat. It has the scientific name Eriogonum jamesii. It was widely used by native Americans in southwestern North America (including Colorado, Utah, Arizona and New Mexico), as a contraceptive. One cup of the root will be consumed by a woman during her period. The meat was chewed, or made into teas to combat depression and stomach aches. It was also used as a pain reliever for childbirth pain. Some eyewashes could be used to treat sore eyes.

Arnica Montana

Native Americans used this member of the sunflower famiy for centuries to apply a cream or ointment topically to ease muscle pains and inflammation. It also helps with sprains, bruises, and wound healing. Arnica can be fatally poisonous so avoid it.

Aspen

Aspen trees can only be found in areas with colder climates and mild summers. This includes both the extreme north-south regions of North America and the high mountain peaks. Quaking Aspen, one of many Aspen types, was used by Native Americans and early settlers to treat inflammation, scurvy cough, pain, swelling, and inflammation. Salicin is a substance that is similar to the active ingredient in aspirin. It can be found in the tree's inner trunk.

Astragalus

Astragalus, a type is astragalus. It is a large genus with approximately 3,000 species. All of these names are familiar: milk-vetch for most species, locoweed for some species in the west United States, and goats'-thorn. To protect against disease, the dried roots were combined with other herbs in Native American and Chinese traditional remedies. There are many traditional medical uses for it. These include colds, pneumonia, anemia and infections as well as stomach ulcers, stomach disorders and hepatitis. It is believed to be helpful in fighting diseases such as diabetes and cancer. It can be used to prevent colds and upper respiratory infection, lower blood pressure, treat diabetes and protect the liver.

Atractylodes

This is a plant belonging to the genus Atractylodes. This herb has long been used in Traditional Medicine for many ailments, including indigestion. Combining it with other herbs can be used to treat certain conditions such as kidney problems and lung cancer.

Bee Pollen

The oldest known health food, this ancient one has been used throughout history by many cultures as a dietary supplement and physical revitalizor. Its tiny seed, which is dust-sized, contains more nutrients than 96 and is found on every flower blossom's stamen. Bees collect it as they move from one flower to the next. It is often collected by placing a device at the entrance of the hive, which brushes pollen from bees' hindlegs into a collection container. It suppresses appetite, improves sexual well-being, treats reproductive issues including PMS, improves digestion, boosts immunity system, improves memory and is also known to aid in hay fever when combined with food beverages. Anaphylactic shock can be experienced by people who are allergic to bee pollen. Avoid bee pollen use if you are allergic to beesstings.

Beeswax

Beeswax comes from the honeycomb of bees. It has been used over centuries for everything, from embalming to candles, creams, and cosmetics. Infold medicine was used in healing salves. Native Americans called the honey bees the "white men's flies", as they were a sign of colonist settlements near them. Wild bees are used by indigenous Americans for hundreds and years. It is still used to make herbal ointments, and to soothe burns. It's said to aid in circulation by dilation of blood vessels. Beeswax cannot be used on the exterior of the body. It can block the intestines and cause intestinal obstruction in those who have consumed it.

Blackberry

Rubus Fruticosus (officially Rubus Fruticosus) is the name given to the root bark, leaves and roots of this plant. These plants have been used for decades to treat various conditions. The root is often used to treat digestive problems, dysentery, and diarrhea. It also helps reduce swelling and stimulates the entire system. You can also use the decoction to treat sores throats, mouth ulcers or gum inflammations.

Nyssa Sylvatica, Or Black Gum

This tree is found throughout eastern North America. It's native from New England and Southern Ontario to central Florida and east Texas. Black Tupelo, Pepperidge and simply Gum or Tupelo are all other names. Native Americans have used the roots, berries, and bark to induce vomiting and cure eye problems. To alleviate chest pain, Cherokee healers used mild tea that was made from small amounts of bark and twigs.

Wild Black Raspberry

Rubus Occidentalis can be called blackcaps or blackcap raspberry, thimbleberry or scotchcap.

When the roots are boiled into tea, or chewed, they can be cathartic. The roots have been used to treat sore eyes as well as ulcers, boils, and sores. The Pawnees and Omaha of the Dakota tribes boiled the root bark to cure dysentery. The roots are extremely astringent and have been traditionally used to treat bowel issues. To treat whooping, a mixture of roots, stems, & leaves is used.

Black Cohosh

Cimicifuga Racosa is the scientific title for this white-flowering Buttercup, which is found in Eastern North America's woods. Black bugbane also goes by the names fairy candle and rattle grass, black snakeroot, and rattlegrass. Native Americans such the Winnebago, Dakota and Oklahoma Delaware knew to use the root in teas to treat gynecological concerns, sore throats. Coughs, headaches and kidney disorders were all treated with the tea. The root's roots were also used to make an alcohol beverage by the Cherokee. During rituals the herb was often mixed together with others and blown on patients. It was then used in sweatbaths. It's still used for gynecological concerns like premenstrual anxieties and menopause, as well aches, nerve disorders, respiratory issues, Tinnitus, Sciatica, and other nervous problems.

Bloodroot

Also known as red puccoon root (or Indian vine), passion, and tetterwort. Native American medicine uses the roots of flowering plants to treat respiratory problems, digestive problems, sore throats, bronchial problems and pain relievers sedatives. They are found in eastern North America's hardwood forests. It was used externally to treat burns, ringworm, and insect repellent. Poultices were made from fresh roots. The plant produces morphine-like amounts of benzylisoquinolinealkaloids, principally the toxin sanguinarine. We now know it is poisonous. Because people have died due to excessive consumption, the Food and Drug Administration has declared it unhealthy. It can also irritate the mucous membranes and cause diarrhea, intestinal colic or vomiting. It has been used by many tribes as a dye, and even the Appalachia Indians as an evil spirit charm.

Cohosh Blue

This flowering plant, previously Caulophyllum Tiltroides, is found in hardwood forests across Canada, from Manitoba to Oklahoma, east to the Atlantic Ocean. Native Americans have been treating a wide range of ailments, including dropsy and colic, cramps as well as hiccough, epilepsy. Also, the source has been used to treat uterine disorders and childbirth pain. Blue Cohosh was used to treat contraception and abortive purposes in many Native American tribes.

Blue Spruce

This is one of the most commonly ornamental conifers. It is stunning with its beautiful silvery blue-green coloring, and perfect Christmas tree shape. Pikes Peak was where the Colorado bluespruce was first discovered in 1862. The popularity of this tree soon spread. It is one of the most popularly planted landscape trees in America. It's stunning and Native Americans have used this tree for centuries for healing. This tree was used by the Navajo, Keres tribes as a traditional healing plant. It also serves as a ritual object for the Keres tribes. Twigs are often given as gifts to bring good luck. It is said that rheumatism symptoms can be treated by infusing needles into a warm bath. Other parts of this tree were used for stomach ailments and colds. Spruce oil is made using the bristly, needlelike spruce leaves and twigs. Native Americans used it to make salves and ointments with honey and alum to treat skin conditions, such as boils, burns or skin irritation. Balsam of pine was also used as glue and caulking. It is still used to treat respiratory issues, cuts, bruises, swelling, pain associated with inflammation, joint pain, and bone pain. Blue Spruce's many components have been used as a disinfectant in homes, furniture polish, insecticide, and air freshener.

Boneset

Eupatorium Perfoliatum also known is a member the asterfamily, which can include up to 60 species. It's also called Eupatorium

Perfoliatum, feverwort or thoroughwort. It is native to temperate North America. It's toxic, but it was used by the Iroquois (Delaware, Cherokee), Mohegan, Menominee, and Mohegan to treat colds. It was used to relieve stomach pains by the Alabama and Cherokee. Due to its high levels of magnesium, calcium, vitamin, niacin, or phosphorus, it has been used for treating dengue fever. To eliminate potential toxic chemicals, tea is usually made with dried leaves instead of fresh. Toxic compounds can damage the liver so use caution. Some side effects include fatigue, muscle tremors, and muscle tremors. In extreme cases, overdose can lead to fatalities.

Boswellia

Frankincense, also known by this name, has been used in traditional medicines for thousands upon thousands of year. It is a species of tree native from India, and its fragrant resin has many pharmacological benefits, including antiinflammatories. It is used to treat asthma, fevers, rheumatisms as well as gastrointestinal problems such depression, arthritis, chronic bronchial disease, ringworms, skin conditions, eczema, stomach ache, jaundice, ringworm, inflammatory bronchial infection, ringworm, skin diseases, and yphilis. It is also used as an expectorant to reduce cholesterol and help people lose weight. Avoid it if you are pregnant, nursing, or with infants.

Broom Snakeweed

Gutierrezia Sarothrae (also known as snakeweed) is a plant from the west and southwest regions of the United States. It was used by Mexicans as well as the Southwestern Indians to treat a number of ailments. The Comanche used it in a decoction to relieve whooping cough. While the Blackfoot boiled and inhaled its steam to treat their respiratory infections, the Blackfoot took the roots out of the boiling water. The Sioux used the steam to treat colds, coughs, and vertigo. Other people used the fresh flowers and roots to treat their skin ailments, such as sores, rheumatism or wounds. It was most commonly used by the Navajo for headaches. It was also used frequently in sweat baths.

Buck Brush

Ceanothus is the scientific title for 50-60 shrubs from North America. The genus only exists in North America. Most species can be found in California, the east United States, Canada and Guatemala. Ceanothus, or "Red Root", is a Native American term that was used to treat cysts. Fibroid tumors, inflammation, throat and mouth problems, as well. It is used for high blood pressure and lymphatic congestion. Hummingbird Blossoms, another Cherokee plant, was used as diuretic to stimulate kidney function. North American tribes used ceanothus intricrimus to assist with childbirth. Ceanothus sanguineus is used to treat swollen tonsils, inflamed tonsils or non-fibrous cysts. Also, it can be used to reduce nervousness, relieve anxiety, treat menstrual bleeding and nosebleeds. Poultices were used in the treatment of burns, sores, wounds and other conditions. The Miwok Indians used Ceanothus to make baskets. In California, early settlers used the plant to replace black tea.

Buckthorn

This is a group of shrubs and trees that belonged to the Rhamnaceae tribe. They are found in the temperate, subtropical Northern Hemisphere, parts of Africa and South America. Buckthorn bark is one of the few parts of the plant that can be used medicinally. Since the 14th Century, Buckthorn bark has been used as an effective laxative or purgative. It is also used to treat liver issues, rheumatisms headaches, allergies and intestinal worms.

Buckwheat

Fagopyrum esculentum, also known as Fagopyrum Esculentum. It is not a grain plant, but rather a high-fiber, manganese, magnesium-rich fruit seed. Despite its bitter flavor, it is used as a herbal remedy and food. It has been used to stop bleeding, treat diarrhea, dysentery or skin lesions and various circulatory issues, as well as to lower blood pressure and improve blood vessel health.

Buffaloberry

Three species of Shepherdia include Canada Buffaloberry Shepherdia Argentea (Shepherdia Canadensis), Russet Buffaloberry Shepherdia Canadensis (Shepherdia Canadensis), Round-leaf Buffaloberry Shepherdia Rothifolia (Shepherdia Rotundifolia). These shrubs are found in North America and Canada. They bear bitter-tasting, small-sized berries. The berries as well as other parts of the plant are known as blueberry, chaparral, chaparral, silverleaf and soopolallie. They have been used long-term as a food, medicine, and dye. The Russet Bufalloberry was one of the most used. It was often used in the making of Indian Ice Cream, a sweet dessert made with hot water, buffaloberries, sugar, and other ingredients. The plant was used to make other beverages, preserves. sauces. dried cakes. Tuberculosis, nausea, vomiting, cystitis, swelling, venereal disease, gastrointestinal problems, fever, fractures, mosquito bites sore eyes, sore throat, sore throat, stomach pain, toothache and gynecological conditions were all treated with parts and berries from the plant. They are edible, but they can cause mouth irritation. The berries can usually be eaten fresh after the first frost has sweetened their natural sweetness. The danger of developing diarrhea can be serious and could lead to death.

Burdock

Also known as Bardana or Cocklebur, this sunflower-related plant is officially called Arctium Lappa. Native Americans adopted the sunflower and continued to use it for centuries, even though it was first found in Eurasia. The roots of the plant have been used in many countries as a vegetable. The Micmac Chippewa and Maliseet tribes provided services like crushing the roots and using them to treat rheumatism. The roots were used to aid in blood circulation and blood purification by the Iroquois. The Potawatomi used the roots to cleanse their blood and make tea. The Indians used it for fruit. They dried its roots to add to soups, and used the young leaves as leaves. It is rich with chromium and iron as well as magnesium, thiamins, phosphorus (vitamin A), zinc, and magnesium. Many tribes used burdock to perform ceremonial functions. Avoid Burdock if youre pregnant or breastfeeding.

Cardinal Flower

This brightly colored, red flowering plant is also known as Lobelia Cardinalis. It can be found in the Americas from southeastern Canada, the eastern and southwest United States, Mexico, Central America, and Central America. Native Americans used the root to treat worms. Leaf tea was used for treating colds, bronchial conditions, nosebleeds (croup), croup, fever, headaches and rheumatism. The roots were used in a poultice to treat painful sores and relieve headaches. The Penobscot tribe made a tobacco replacement using the dried leaves. The Lobelia family considers it potentially toxic, although the extent of the toxicity is still unknown. The sap from the plant can cause skin irritation.

Cascara Sagrada

Rhamnus Purshiana (also known as Rhamnus Purshiana) is a buckthorn-tree that's native to west North America. It ranges from southern British Columbia to central California to inland to western Montana. Cascara Buckthorn Bark, Chitticum Bark Bark and Sacred Bark are used to treat bowel problems. It has a strong laxative action and is thought that it can improve the muscle tone in the colon walls. It can also be made from dried bark. However, the tea has a bitter flavor. Fresh cascara bark should not be used as it can cause bloody vomiting and diarrhea. It should be aged at the least for one year and subject to heat treatment.

Catnip/Catmint

Also known as catswort, it is officially called Nepeta cataria. Despite being from Europe, Asia, Africa, the herb is now well-known in North America. The herb's calming properties and mild numbing properties have been used for centuries in medicine. It can be used to make teas, poultices, or smoke it. To make aromatic herb tea, you can use fresh or dried stems or leaves. This herbal tea effectively treats digestive disorders, lowers fever, treats infant colic and treats colds, flu and colds. It has also been proven to be helpful in the treatment and prevention of anxiety, restlessness, and other symptoms. The leaves can also be used externally to make salves, which are applied to bruises, and especially to black eyes. Season salads with raw, young leaves that have a minty flavor are common. The oil extracted from this plant has been shown to repel rodents, insects, and rats.

Cat's Claw

Also known as Cat's Nail. Officially, it is Uncaria Tomentosa. It has been used for more than 2 000 years as a general tonic, contraceptive and anti-inflammatory agent, digestive and urinary tract issues and diarrhea, as well as for respiratory problems, skin conditions, diabetes and respiratory problems. It grows in South America and Asia's rainforests, jungles, and mountains. Research suggests that it could positively affect and improve the immune systems and treat cancers such as diabetes, PMS (chronic fatigue syndrome), prostate disorders, and Aids.

Cayenne:

Capsicum can be called Chili Pepper, Red Pepper and Tabasco Pepper. It is an American native, and has been cultivated in the Americas for thousands of year by tropical peoples. Today it is grown throughout the world. It was first used to treat circulatory and digestive problems. The other conditions it was used to treat were: rheumatism; arthritis; chronic nerve pain; shingles; diabetes; stomach problems; varicose veins; headaches; menstrual cramps and asthma. It was also used to soothe throat irritation by gargling. Externally, it was used for improving blood supply and to numb wound pain. It is now used to treat high blood cholesterol and high blood sugar.

Chamomile:

This plant, which looks like a daisy, is well-known for its ability make a wide range of teas to aid sleep. They can be used to treat gynecologic disorders like PMS and cramps. It is safe for both babies and children, and also acts as a great calming agent.

Chasteberry:

Vitex Agnus–catus is the official name of the Chaste fruit. It has been used for many years to reduce the effects of menstrual disorders and promote breast milk growth. It was also known under the names chaste-tree berry, vitex and monks pepper. It was believed that monks used it in Middle Ages to curb sexual appetites and preserve its purity. Now it is clear that the herb has no effect on sex drive. Teas made with berries and flowers can be used for PMS, infertility, breast problems, PMS, menopause symptoms, PMS, PMS, PMS, PMS, PMS and other conditions. It has been proven to be both an anti-inflammatory and for bone strength and epilepsy. Avoid taking the chasteberry if you are pregnant or breastfeeding.

Chokecherry

Also known as Black Chokecherry or Western Chokecherry. Prunus Virginiana is its scientific name. There are several types of Prunus Virginiana in the United States as well as Canada. Many tribes depend on trees for food or medicine. It was also considered to be one of the most useful native medicines in early American treatment. The berries could be harvested and dried for later consumption. Smallpox was also used for soreness of the neck and chest, as well as for scurvy, scurvy. Europeans discovered the health benefits of chokeberry when they arrived to America. You could use it for everything: colds, flu, malaria, burns, wounds, and even consumption. The colors of the fruits vary from red, purple, black and there are slight variations. Although the berries can still be eaten, the pits can be dangerous if taken in large quantities.

Chlorella

One-celled green alga has the potential to prevent cancer, improve immune system support, manage weight, lower blood pressure, lower cholesterol, and speed up wound healing.

Chickweed

Stellaria Pubera and Stellaria Media, also known as the Stellaria Media plant, was originally found in Eurasia. It can be found in North America from Alaska's Brooks Range down to the continent's southernmost tip. Chickweeds have been used for medicine and food, including Star Chickweed (Common Chickweed), and Mouse-ear Chickweed. The whole plant, which contains high levels of vitamins and minerals has been used to treat constipation. Poultices are used to treat rheumatic conditions, such as rashes, wounds.

Cinnamon Bark

Cinnamon comes from the inner barks of many trees belonging the genus Cinnamomum. These trees are native to Southeast Asia. It has been in use for over 4,000years and is even listed in the Bible. It is well-known for its many medical applications in different cultures. It has been used over the years to improve cognitive function and memories, treat rheumatisms, colds. diabetes. toothaches. It is believed that drinking tea made with Sri Lanka cinnamon bark can reduce the chances of getting oxidative-related illnesses.

Cloves:

Syzygium aromaticum, which is the official name for these aromatic dried flower buds are native to Indonesia. They are used as a spice or medicinal remedy. Some of its uses include heartburn, bad breath and cough, as well as toothache, bad taste, skin infection, gum problems, stomach issues, flatulence, nausea and heartburn. It also has antioxidant effects.

Coneflower.

Gossypium is the home of cotton, a subtropical tropical plant that is found in Africa, Asia, and India. All sorts of problems such as heavy bleeding, urination, burns or dysentery have been treated using roots, leaves and seeds. Alabama and Koasati tribes prepared tea from the roots of plants to alleviate labor pains.

Creosote Bush:

Larrea Tridentata the official name for this plant. However, it is often called "chaparral", as it is a medicinal herb. It's quite common in the south deserts. Native Americans in Southwest America brewed tea from the leaves. It was used among other purposes to treat respiratory problems, sexually transmitted disorders, tuberculosis or snakebite. The United States Food and Drug Administration released warnings about the risks of ingesting chaparral, claiming it can cause liver and renal damage.

Damiana

This small shrub, which is aromatic, is found in the southwestern United States, California, Mexico, South America, South America, South America, and Caribbean. It is officially called Turnera Diffusa. It has been used for centuries to stimulate libido. It can be used to treat depression, impotence and anxiety as well as constipation.

Dandelion:

Taraxacum Officinale is the official name. It is most well-known as a weed. But herbalists treasure it for its numerous culinary as well as medicinal uses. Its leaves and roots are high in vitamins C, B complex, and D. They also contain minerals like iron and potassium. The roots of the Dandelion are used in coffee replacements. Some wines are made from its flowers. The roots and the leaves of the Dandelion were used as herbal medicine to treat liver disease, kidney failure and swelling. They also helped with stomach problems such as heartburn, skin problems, skin problems, liver problems, kidney damage, skin issues, heartburn, and stomach problems. The Pillager Ojibwas had heartburn and the Mohegan tribe had tea made from the root. The Chinese used it to treat heartburn, stomach problems, and appendicitis. It was used in Europe by herbalists to treat diseases such as fevers and boils, eye problems, diabetes, and dizziness. Today, the roots of Dandelion are used as an appetite stimulant.

Dogwood:

Cornus Florida refers to the name of the flowering tree found throughout the United States. The tree can be found anywhere from Maine to Florida west to Minnesota, Kansas and Texas. Native American remedies include the use of the American Dogwood's inner bark and berries as well as its twigs and berries.

It was used to treat symptoms such as malaria, influenza, coughs, and nausea, as well increasing appetite and digestion. Poultices can be applied externally to treat sores and ulcers. In the early 1800s, Virginia Native Americans were famous for their whiter teeth. They chewed on twigs that served as both a toothpick, and a toothbrush.

The Cherokee chewed the bark to ease headaches. To treat childhood illnesses like measles, worms, and diarrhea, the Iroquois used the leaves in a tonic to combat gonorrhea. Poultices could also be made to treat burns or other skin conditions. The Arikara combined the bark with bearberry to make sacred tobacco. Menominees also used it for enemas. It was popularly used in the South for chronic diarrhea and malarial fever treatment during the Civil War.

Dong Quai:

Angelica Sinensis has been used tonic medicine China Korea and Japan for over 1,000 years. It was used traditionally in traditional medicine to treat fertility issues such as PMS and cramps. Also, it increased circulation and eased menopausal symptoms. It has also been shown that it can help with chronic or persistent nasal or sinus congestion and fibroid tumors. It can also dilate blood vessels and activate and relax uterine tissues, according to research.

Eastern Skunk Cabbage

This is also known for Clumpfoot Cabbage. It's a very low-growing plant with a foul-smelling scent. This plant can be found in the wild across the eastern United States from Minnesota to North Carolina and Tennessee. It was used widely by the Winnebago tribes and Dakota tribes to relieve asthmatic symptoms such as phlegm withdrawal. It was also used as a magic talisman by various tribes. It was used from 1820-1882 as a medication called "dracontium" to treat respiratory ailments, nervous disorders, and dropsy. They should not be consumed raw as the roots are poisonous, and the leaves can cause severe burns to the mouth. However, you can dry the leaves and use them in soups or stews.

Elder

Officially, the Sambucus genus includes tall shrubs as well as small trees belonging to the Honeysuckle Family. While there are many species native to North America and Europe of Honeysuckle, the Sambucus Canadensis, also known as Black Elderberry, is North America's most well-known tribe. Elderberries are used both as food and in herbal treatment as soon as they ripen.

The berries can be used to make food and drink syrups, fruit drinks that are made with water and alcohol, as well wine and alcoholic beverages. Traditional herbal medicine used berries and dried flower tonics in teas and other remedies for constipation. The Cherokee and Delaware used dried flowers to make tea to flush out contaminants. The Seminole and Creek made a paste from the root, which they used as a topical swelling-relieving remedy.

The Houma Indians used berries to make tonic, and the Ponca, Iroquois and Dakota tribes used them to make a refreshing drink for summer. To make hollow tubes for flutes, whistles, bow shafts, skewers and toys in spring, tree branches were removed from the trees. However, this is not recommended due the potential for cyanide poisoning. Avoid unripe fruit as they may contain poisonous alkaloids. There is also a cyanide compound in the roots, leaves and twigs. It is best to avoid excessive consumption in order to avoid dangerous accumulations of cyanide.

Eleuthero:

Eleutherococcus Senticosus can be described as a small, woody shrub. It is native to Northeastern Asia. It is also found in southeastern Siberia. It's also known under the names Siberian Ginseng and Devil's Bush, Devil's Shrub or Pepperbrush, Prickly Eleutherococcus (also Touch-Me-Not and Wild Pepper), which has been used in herbal medicines since 190 A.D. The dried roots can be used to treat symptoms such as flu, weakness, and swelling. They also improve concentration, focus, strength, endurance, and immunity system. If you are on medication for high cholesterol, consult your doctor before taking this medicine. You should take it at least an hour before bed to avoid sleeping problems.

Evening Primrose

Oenothera or Onagraceae is the official name of a genus with around 125 flowering plant species that is native to North America and

South America. Suncups or Sundrops are another name for it. This plant has been used as both a vegetable and as a remedy for herbal ailments for many years. The shoots and peppery young roots are edible as vegetables.

The whole plant could be used in decoctions to relieve pain, asthma, and cough. Poultices can also be used for swelling, cuts, and wound healing. The Apache used it to make soups and sauces. While the Cherokee cooked the roots as potatoes, the Cherokee roasted the leaves and boiled them for their greens.

Hopi, Navajo and Jemez used the heart for ceremonial medicine. Ramah and Navajo used it for muscle pain and swelling as well as throat problems; the Blackfoot used this for sores. Hopi and Hopi also used it to treat eye conditions. Cherokees used it for a range of purposes, including for hemorhoid, boils, strength, and to limit "over fatness".

Fendler's Bladderpod:

Officially Lesquerella fendleri. A genus of flowering plants in the mustard family. Native

Americans including the Hopi used the root to treat snakebite, induce vomiting, and provide gynecological care during childbirth. Kayenta and Navajo tribes applied the seeds to sore eyes. The Navajo also used the seeds to clean their noses, crush leaves to alleviate toothaches and bites, as well as to make a snuff.

Fennel

This herb is very aromatic and flavourful. It has been used for centuries in medicine and cooking. It was originally found on the Mediterranean coasts but spread across the globe. Spanish missionaries brought the plant to North America in order to make it available for English settlers and their medicinal gardens. Puritan folk medicine used it as a digestive aid. The seeds, leaves, roots, and essential oil of fennel can all be eaten. However, it is possible to get poisonous levels from small amounts. It has been used for many purposes, including as a digestive aid, flatulence cure, appetite stimulant, increased breast milk flow in breastfeeding mothers, and to increase breast size. Teas and herbal tonics from the leaves and seeds were used to treat nausea, colic, constipation and other ailments such as colds, asthma, respiratory problems, stomach cramps, and baby colic. The external application of poultices to sore eyes was done using externally applied wash. The Hopi tribe used the plant to substitute tobacco.

Feverwort:

Horse Gentian is also known as Fever-root and Wild Coffee Tinker's weed. This course, leafy herb belongs to the honeysuckle family. Officially, it is Triosteum Perfoliatum. It has been used over many years for the treatment of nausea, vomiting and itching, as well as anxiety symptoms, joint pain, back pain, itching, pleurisy and joint discomfort. A decoction from the plant was brewed by the Cherokee to treat their fever. Boneset also has a name, Feverwort.

Gentiana

This is a genus with over 400 species and it belongs to Gentianaceae. This plant is characterized by Bitter Root (or Bitter Wort),

Gal Weed (or Gal Weed), Yellow Gentian, Sampsons Snakeroot (or Longdan), and Qin Jiao. You can find most species in alpine habitats. Despite its bitter taste and widespread use by Native Americans, it was used to treat digestive problems and stimulate appetite. Many species were used to eradicate worms and treat Malaria. It was also used topically as a treatment for wounds and painful inflammation. One tribe, Catawba Indians soaked the roots in hot water and applied it to their sore backs. Consuming gentian can irritate your ulcers and cause headaches.

Geranium:

With around 200 varieties available in different parts of the world, Geraniums is one of the Pelargonium genera. Stork's Bill is another common name for this plant. Teas made of scented geranium plants were traditionally used in folk medicine to treat stomach ulcers and headaches. To heal children with thrush, Native American medicine used a combination made up of wild grape and boiling geranium root. The Chippewa, Ottawa and other tribes boiled whole plants of geranium to treat diarrhea. They then drank this tea.

Goldenrod

Solidago Canadensis (or Solidago Virgaurea) has been used for years as a topical healer. It can also be used to treat conditions such as diabetes, tuberculosis (liver enlargement), hemorrhoids, internal bleeding and asthma. It is antimicrobial and antiinflammatory, so it can be used to treat infection.

Goldenseal

Hydrastis Canadensis is also known as Yellow Root (or Orange Root), Puccoon (or Ground Raspberry), and Wild Curcuma. Native Americans used it as a stimulant and to treat eye irritations, stomach issues, liver problems, and stomach problems. It's native to the southeast of Canada and the northeastern United States. The Cherokee used bear fat to protect themselves from insects by pounding large rootstocks with it. The Iroquois first introduced the herb for medicinal purposes to early colonists. It has also been used for throat, sinus, throat and intestines as well as vaginal infections and mild wound healing. Goldenseal is not recommended for pregnant women.

Grapefruit

This is a subtropical orange tree with a bitter flavor that is widely grown all over the world. Its inner rind, seeds, and pulp have been shown to fight both bacterial as well as fungal infections. It is an excellent source of nutrients that contributes to a healthy diet. Grapefruit has high levels of vitamin C and antioxidants. Research suggests that it may reduce cholesterol, prevent kidney stone formation, and protect from colon cancer. Grapefruit peel can treat stomach aches with vitamins and minerals. Grapefruit seed oil has been used as an anti-septic when people travel to areas where the water quality is questionable. It aids the kidneys in cleansing themselves. It is used among other things to treat muscle weakness or stiffness, acne and fluid retention.

Greenbriar

Smilax Bona Nox, a larger Smilax family that includes more than 300 species, is officially the Smilax Bona Nox. Bullbar is also known as Horsebriar (Catbriar), Horsebriar (Prickly-ivys), and Pull Out a Sticker To the Cherokee. This plant can be found all over the globe in temperate, tropic, and subtropical areas. Many of these woody and toughy roots are used as diuretics to treat urinary problems and dropsy. The roots have been used to heal rheumatism and stomach ailments. Stem prickles are used as a remedy for localized pains, cramps and twitching. Also, poultices and balms made from leaves and bark were used to treat minor sores, burns, boils, and other conditions. Sarsaparilla comes from the Smilax tribe, which is much more well-known.

Guarana

The Amazonian climbing plants contain caffeine. This plant is used commonly as a mild stimulant. It has been used, among others, to treat headaches. It activates the nervous and gives you more control. In the past, it was also used to combat malaria and other diseases like dysentery.

Gymnema Sylvestre

This herb from India's tropical forests has been used to treat diabetes for over 2,000 years. The whole plant, also known by Cowplant, can help with digestive problems, constipation.

NATIVE AMERICAN HEALING METHODS

Native Americans have used herbs to bring healing to the body and spirit for thousands of years. According to oral traditions they learned about herbs' healing power and other plants by observing sick animals. The history of America's native peoples' medicinal use is not documented before the Europeans encountered them. However, Native Americans began to share their knowledge of natural remedies with the Europeans.

Native American remedies utilized hundreds of herbs and plant species, but tobacco was considered the most sacred. It was used in rituals, ceremonies, and treatment of a number of illnesses. It was smoked raw, with no additives.

Native Americans believed Sage was an important herb because it could treat a number of ailments including stomach, colon, liver, kidneys and liver.

While the variety of medicinal herbs contained in a Healer's medicine pack is extensive, the most popular were the ones that were used the most. These included remedies for common colds (American Ginseng, Boneset), herbs to relieve aches and pains (Wild Black Cherry, Pennyroyal and Hops), and fever remedies (Dogwood, Feverwort and Willow Bark).

Cramps/Abdominal Pain:

The cattail plant is used in both internal and external medicine.

Galangal is a ginger related herb that can be used for digestive issues. It is similar to other ginger-related herbal remedies.

Sage is used in cooking for thousands and has been used since ancient times. Similar to other culinary herbs, it has been long considered a digestive aid as well as an appetite stimulant.

* Saw Palmetto is a long-cherished food source that Native Americans have used to make baskets and fans as well as for medicinal purposes.

* Abortifacient - A substance that prevents an individual from having an abortion.

* Pennyroyal is used for treating medical problems and pests. Women who are pregnant should not use pennyroyal. Overdosing with this herb can lead to death.

Rosemary is a herb used in both cooking, and medicine.

* Native Americans used skullcap for a variety of medicinal purposes. Do not give skullcap to pregnant women.

* Native Americans used slippery alm for many purposes.

Abscesses

* Burdock- Both the roots and the leaves of this plant can be used externally and internally. Stay away from this plant if youre pregnant or nursing.

* Devil's Claw (Internally, it's used to make teas and tinctures, and externally, in poultices. This product is not recommended for women who are, or could become pregnant.

* Echinacea's roots can be chewed, dried in tea, or pulverized externally.

* Chamomile is a herb that is often used in teas. It is best known for its ability to help with sleep.

* Pau d'arco has for many years been used to treat a variety if ailments.

* Poke: Although some parts of this plant are toxic to livestock and humans it has been used by Native Americans for food and medicine for many years.

Native Americans use the inner bark, young leaves, pitch, and twigs of white Pine for herbal remedies.

* Native Americans used slippery alm for many purposes.

* Wild Yam has always been used both as medicine and food.

Aches, pains and discomforts

* Black Cohosh Tea - Teas made with the roots of the plant have been used to treat many ailments.

* Osha Native Americans highly revere OSHA for its many medicinal properties.

* Saltbush can be used for a wide range of ailments.

Acne

* Buffaloberry is a fruit that can be eaten and used for herbal remedies. Overindulgence can result in severe consequences, including death.

* Burdock- Both the roots and the leaves of this plant can be used externally and internally. Stay away from this plant if youre pregnant or breastfeeding.

* Cat's Claw was used in teas and tonics.

Chasteberry is a tea made of berries and flowers. Chasteberry is not recommended for pregnant women or those who are nursing.

* Dandelion plants can be used as both medicinal and food ingredients.

* Lavender: Lavender has been used as a tea, balm, food, or herbal remedy since Roman times.

* Mint-Dried leaves for teas and other foods that are helpful in a variety healing methods.

Red Clover has long been used to treat a wide range of conditions.

* Sarsaparilla has been used for many herbal treatments over the years.

* American Indians used witchhazel extensively for their medicinal purposes.

* Yellow Dock was used as traditional medicine by Native Americans.

ADHD (Attention Deficit Hyperactivity Disorder).

* Ginkgo Biloba- This tree, one of the oldest on the planet, has been used to provide food and medicinal purposes for thousands of year.

* Lavender: Lavender has been used as a tea, balm, food, or herbal remedy since Roman times.

Oat Straw has been used for both food and medicinal purposes.

* Skullcap is a potent herbal remedy that can be used in a variety medicinal treatments. Avoid skullcap use by pregnant women.

* St. John's Wort (or St. John's Wort) is an herb that can be used to treat various ailments. It is most well-known for its antidepressant properties, but it can also be used in other medical settings.

Allergies

* Dong Quai can be used to treat a number of conditions for more than a thousand years.

* Mint – These dried leaves can be used to make teas or foods that are beneficial for various ailments.

* Rooibos – Rooibos Tea is used for several conditions.

* For many years, goldenrod has been used to treat a variety of ailments.

* Spirulina -- Spirulina can be described as a type blue-green alga rich in vitamins and proteins.

Alzheimer's Disease

* Ginkgo Biloba- This tree, one of the oldest on the planet, has been used to provide food and medicinal purposes for thousands of year.

Anemia

* Dong Quai can be used to treat many conditions for more than a thousand years.

* Senna is a large group of flowering plants from the genus Senna that has been used in a variety remedies.

* Wheat Grass- This grass is used to treat many medical conditions. It has been cultivated over the past decades.

Antibiotics

* Ashwagandha-The whole plant can be used in many different treatments. It should be treated with caution as it is poisonous.

Antibacterial:

* Fenugreek herb can be used externally and internally to treat various ailments.

* The inner rind, pulp, and grapefruit seeds can all be used to treat internal diseases.

* Teas, tonics and salves made from horsemint leaf and flowering stems can be used to treat a wide variety of ailments. Avoid it for pregnant women.

* Lavender: Lavender has been used as a tea, balm, and food ingredient since Roman times.

Pinon: This was the Native American term for Pinon, which was widely used by Native

Americans. Some tribes have called it the "tree that gives life."

* The younger pads of the pear Cactus were used for food and tea by the Abrasive Native Americans, while the more mature pads were used in poultices.

* Goldenrod stiff - This herb has been used longtime to treat bleeding, and other ailments.

* Sumac: Sumac was sacred to some peoples. It was used for medicine and food.

* White Willow - Willow bark is used for thousands of year.

Antioxidant

* Ginkgo Biloba- This tree, one of the oldest on the planet, has been used to provide food and medicinal purposes for thousands of year.

* The inner rind, pulp, and grapefruit seeds can all be used to treat internal diseases.

* Olive Oil, a tree crop popular in Mediterranean countries, has been used in medicine and food for hundreds of years.

* Sarsaparilla has been used for many herbal treatments over the years.

* Schisandra is one genus which includes shrubs with wide-ranging medicinal properties.

* Spirulina -- Spirulina can be described as a type blue-green alga rich in vitamins and proteins.

* White Willow - Willow bark is used for thousands of year.

Anxiety

* Damiana internally is used to treat multiple ailments.

* Hops are best-known for being used in beer but also have medicinal properties.

* Kava Kava is a folk medicine that has been enjoyed for thousands of year.

Kola nut is a well-known herb that has been used for centuries in spiritual practices and ceremonial rituals. You should not use it if you're pregnant or nursing.

* Lavender: Lavender has been used as a tea, balm, food, or herbal remedy since Roman times.

* Since the Middle Ages lemon balm has served as a soothing herb.

* Passion Flower: This flower is a traditional Native American herb, which was adopted by European colonists in the early days of European settlement. Passionflower should never be consumed if you are pregnant, nursing, or otherwise ill.

* Peppermint is a long-standing herbal medicine ingredient that has been used for its soothing and numbing qualities, as well flavoring. This product should be avoided by infants and children.

* Rhodiola Rosea. Rhodiola Rosea's well-known ability to improve mental and physical abilities is known.

* Native Americans cultivated skullcap for medicinal purposes. Do not give skullcap to pregnant women.

* St John's Wort is an herb that is most commonly used in antidepressants, but it also has other medical uses.

* Valerian Root: Valerian Root has long been used as a healing herb in ancient Greece and Rome.

* Wild Lettuce is a North American native that was traditionally used to sedate nervous conditions.

Aphrodisiacs

* Damiana internally can be used to treat various ailments. Guarana, which contains caffeine, has many of these same effects as coffee.

* Savory: An aromatic herb used in folk medicines and as a flavoring agent.

Appendicitis

* Dandelion plants can be used as both medicinal and food ingredients.

Stimulant for Appetite

* Devil's Claw (Internally, it's used to make teas and tinctures, and externally it's used to make poultices. This product is not recommended for women who are, or might become pregnant.

* Bark, seeds, twigs, and seeds of dogwood can all be used in external and internal decoctions.

* Fennel has leaves, seeds, and roots which can be used in medicine and cooking. Fenugreek herb can be used externally and internally to treat various ailments.

* Gentiana (or bitter) is a herb that is used to treat external and internal problems. Inflammation, headaches and nausea can all be symptoms of ulcers.

* Ginger root is used around the world as a seasoning or medicine.

* Horehound is an herb that can be used externally and internally. Peptic ulcer and gastritis sufferers should avoid using it.

* Lemon balm has been used since the Middle Ages as a soothing herb.

* Rabbit Tobacco -- Many Indians believed this to possess mystical or magical properties.

Sage has been used in culinary arts for thousands upon thousands of years. Like other culinary herbs, it is considered a digestive aid as well as an appetite stimulant.

* Saw Palmetto is a long-cherished food source that Native Americans used to make baskets and fans. It also has medicinal properties.

* Star anise (a small tree whose fruits have a licorice like taste) has been used in medical remedies for many years.

* The dried bark of wild black cherry was used to make syrups and teas for various ailments.

* Wild garlic is used for medicinal and culinary purposes throughout history.

* Native Americans used wild ginger root as a medicine plant and as a spice.

* Wormwood-The flowers and leaves from this plant were dried and collected for use as tonics.

Appetite Suppressant

* Bee Pollen is one among man's oldest food sources. It can be found in foods and beverages as well as in pill supplements.

* Dandelion plants can be used as both medicinal and food ingredients.

Garcinia Cambogia is a fruit-rind extract that can be used in a number of ways. Garcinia Cambogia should not be used by people suffering from diabetes, dementia, and pregnant or lactating women.

Guarana can have many of the same effects that coffee, because it contains caffeine.

Kola nut is a well-known herb that has been used for centuries in spiritual practices and ceremonial rituals. You should not use it if you're pregnant or nursing.

* Yerba Mate Holly species has a long history in medicinal herbs.

Arthritis

* Alfalfa- A food additive that is used for a variety of medicinal purposes. You should avoid any auto-immune condition.

* Black Cohosh Tea - Teas made with the roots of the plant have been used to treat many ailments.

* Boneset Tea - This is tea made from dried leaf. It can be dangerous and have side effects, so please use caution.

* Boswellia -- A fragrant resin that can be used to treat many conditions. This product should be avoided by both pregnant and nursing mothers as well as children.

* Buffaloberry is a fruit that can be eaten and used for herbal remedies. Overindulgence can result in severe consequences, including death.

* Devil's Claw (Internally, it's used to make teas and tonics. Externally, it's used for poultices. Use it if your are pregnant or believe you may be.

* Eucalyptus Teas and Ointments for a Wide Range of Uses

* Feverfew: This herb can be used for several internal medical issues. Pregnant women should not use it.

* Ginger root is used around the world as a seasoning or medicine.

* For many years, goldenrod has been used to treat a variety of ailments.

* Green Tea – This is the Camellia Sinensis tea that is made only from Camellia Sinensis plants leaves. It has many health benefits.

* Greenbriar- External and internal use of teas, salves and greenbriar.

Guarana can have many of the same effects that coffee, because it contains caffeine.

* Juniper is a herb that can be used internally and externally. Because of the risk of miscarriage, pregnant women should avoid this herb.

* Osha Native Americans highly revere OSHA due its wide variety of medicinal properties.

* For many years, Pau d'arco was used to treat a variety if ailments.

* Poke: Although some parts of this plant are toxic to livestock and humans it has been used

by Native Americans for food and medicine for many years.

* Sarsaparilla has been used for many herbal treatments over the years.

* Shavegrass has long been used as an effective treatment for a number of ailments.

* Native Americans used slippery alm for many purposes.

* Seeds of stoneseed can be used for a number of medical conditions.

Native Americans use the inner bark, young leaves, pitch, and twigs of white Pine for herbal remedies.

* Wild garlic is used for both medicinal and culinary purposes throughout history.

* Yellow Dock was used as traditional medicine by Native Americans.

Asthma

* Boswellia -- A fragrant resin that can be used to treat many conditions. This product is not

recommended to be used on pregnant and nursing mothers or children.

* Coltsfoot: This dandelion-like weed has been used for medicinal purposes for thousands of year for various purposes throughout the world.

* Damiana internally is used to treat multiple ailments.

* Eastern Skunk Cabbage -- Dried leaves used in various tribes for medicinal purposes and magic talismans.

* Afternoon Primrose Decoctions were used internally and externally for various ailments.

* Feverfew: This herb can be used for several internal medical problems. Pregnant women should not use it.

* For many years, goldenrod has been used to treat a variety of ailments.

* Honeysuckle – For thousands upon years, honeysuckle is used in traditional herbal remedies.

* Horehound is an herb that can be used externally and internally. Peptic ulcer and gastritis sufferers should avoid using it.

* Indian hemp is a variety of marijuana. It's used to make clothes, paper, and medicinal teas.

Kola nuts are used in traditional herbal and spiritual treatments. You should not use it if you're pregnant or nursing.

* Lemongrass has been used for its antifungal property as a pesticide and a preservative.

* Mullein is an herb-like tobacco plant, which has a long history as a medicinal remedy.

* Poke: Although some parts of this plant are toxic to livestock and humans it has been used by Native Americans for many years as food, medicine, and fuel.

* Rabbit Tobacco -- Many Indians believed it to have mystical or mystic qualities.

* Rooibos – Rooibos Tea is used for several conditions.

* Sumac: Sumac was sacred to some peoples. It was used for medicine and food.

* The dried bark of wild black cherry was used in syrups and teas to treat various diseases.

* Wild garlic is used for medicinal and culinary purposes throughout history.

* Native Americans used the roots from wild ginger both as a spice, and as a healing plant.

* Wild Onion's use as a medicine or food has a long history.

* Since thousands years, yarrow has been used as a way to stop bleeding.

Astringent.

* The inner rind, pulp, and grapefruit seeds can all be used to treat internal diseases.

* Raspberry fruits and leaves can be used to treat a wide range of illnesses.

* Rose Hips - Since centuries, teas made from the rosehip plant have been used to treat many ailments.

* Goldenrod stiff - This herb has been used longtime to treat bleeding, and other ailments.

* Sumac: Sumac was sacred to some peoples. It was used for medicine and food.

* Yarrow has long been used to stop bleeding.

Back pain

* Arnica is not recommended for use topically. It can be poisonous if consumed internally.

* Devil's Claw (Internally, it's used to make teas and tonics. Externally, it's used for poultices. You should not use it if pregnant or thinking about becoming pregnant. Feverwort can both be used internally and externally.

* Gentiana (or bitter) is a herb that is used to treat external and internal problems. People with ulcers may suffer from inflammation as well as nausea, vomiting, headaches, and nausea.

* Teas, tonics and salves made from horsemint leaf and flowering stems can be used to treat a variety od ailments. Pregnant or nursing women should not use it.

* Milkweed: Milkweed is a plant that can be used to make string, ropes, and other materials. Milkweed can cause poison if it is not prepared properly.

Bed-wetting:

* Persimmons-This fruit has a long history as a food or traditional medicine. The treatment of a number of ailments has been treated with shave grass for decades.

* Sumac: Sumac was sacred to some peoples. It was used for medicine and food.

Bladder problems:

* Alfalfa- A food additive that is used for a variety of medicinal purposes. You should avoid any auto-immune condition.

* For many years, goldenrod has been used to treat a variety of ailments.

* Goldenseal is an herb that can be used internally and externally. It is best to avoid it for pregnant women.

* Juniper is a herb that can be used internally and externally. Because of the risk of miscarriage, pregnant women should avoid this herb.

* Lemongrass has been used for its antifungal property as a pesticide and a preservative.

* Native Hemlock – Native Americans used it as an herbal dye, to make baskets and wooden objects, and for medicinal purposes.

* Oak: The bark and acorns from the oak tree are used to treat many ailments.

* Shavegrass has long been used to treat a variety of illnesses.

* Stoneseed seed can be used for a number of medical conditions.

* Sumac: Sumac was sacred to some people. It was used for medicine and food.

* Uva Ursi can be used to treat a variety of ailments. It has been around since the second millennium. It is best to avoid it for pregnant women.

* You can use carrots (wild and domesticated) to treat a variety ailments.

* Wild roses of all varieties have been used for medicinal purposes for thousands of years.

Controlling Bleeding

* Green Tea – This is the Camellia Sinensis tea that is made only from Camellia Sinensis plants leaves. It has many health benefits.

* Native Hemlock – Native Americans used it for dyeing their skins, making baskets and wood items, and medicinal purposes.

* Native Americans used younger pads from the prickly Pear cactus for tea and food, while the mature pads were used as poultices.

Sage has been used in culinary arts for thousands upon thousands of years. Like other culinary herbs, it is considered a digestive aid as well as an appetite stimulant.

* Shavegrass has long been used to treat a variety of illnesses.

* Goldenrod stiff - This herb has been used longtime to treat bleeding, and other ailments.

* American Indians used witchhazel extensively for their medicinal purposes.

Bloating

* Ginger root is used around the world as a seasoning or medicine.

Lemon balm has been used since the Middle Ages as a soothing herb.

Sage has been used in cooking since thousands of years. Like other culinary herbs, it is considered a digestive aid as well as an appetite stimulant.

* Uva Ursi can be used to treat a variety of ailments. It has been around since the second millennium. Avoid it for pregnant women.

Clotting of Blood:

* Alfalfa- A food additive that is used for a variety of medicinal purposes. You should avoid any auto-immune condition.

* Buckwheat – The fruit seed was used to supplement herbal remedies.

Blood Pressure

* Buck Brush is an umbrella term for a group North American shrubs, which are used in herbal medicines.

* Buckwheat – The fruit seed was used to supplement herbal remedies.

* Dong Quai can be used to treat a number of conditions for more than a thousand years.

* Ginkgo Biloba- This tree, one of the oldest on the planet, has been used to provide food and medicinal purposes for thousands of year.

* Ginger root is used around the world as a seasoning or medicine.

* Hibiscus: There are many types and varieties of hibiscus. They have been used in traditional herb medicine since Roman times.

* Honeysuckle – For thousands upon years honeysuckle is used in traditional herbal remedies.

* Juniper is a herb that can be used internally and externally. Because of the risk of miscarriage, pregnant women should avoid this herb.

* Jiaogulan, a Chinese herb that is well-known for its anti-aging properties and many health benefits.

* Mint-Dried leaves for teas and food that are helpful in a variety healing methods.

* Persimmons - This fruit has a long tradition of being used in traditional medicine and as food.

* Schisandra is one genus which includes shrubs with many medicinal properties.

* The dried bark of wild black cherry was often used in syrups and teas to treat various ailments.

* Wild garlic is used for both medicinal and culinary purposes throughout history.

* Yellow root - Native Americans used it to make tea for various ailments, even though it's toxic in large quantities.

* Yerba Mate Holly species has a long history in medicinal herbs.

Circulatory Health

* Buffaloberry is a berry that can be eaten and used for herbal remedies. Overindulgence can result in severe consequences, including death

* Burdock- Both the roots and the leaves of this plant can be used externally and internally. Stay away from this plant if youre pregnant or breastfeeding.

* The cattail is an herb that can be used as a vegetable or in internal and exterior medicine.

* Dandelion plants can be used as both medicinal and food ingredients.

* Devil's Claw (Internally, it's used to make teas and tonics. Externally, it's used to make poultices. This product is not recommended for women who are, or may become, pregnant.

* Fenugreek herb can be used externally and internally to treat various ailments.

* Chamomile is a herb that is often used in teas. It is best known for aiding with sleep.

* Greenbriar- External and internal use of teas, salves and greenbriar.

* Marshmallow Root: This root has long been used as a food and medicinal remedy.

* Passion Flower: Native Americans used this flower for many years, and European colonists later adopted it. Passionflower should never be consumed if you're pregnant, nursing, or otherwise ill.

* Native Americans used younger pads of the pikly pear cactus for tea and food, while the mature pads were used as poultices.

* Pau d'arco has for many years been used to treat a variety if ailments.

* Native Americans used slippery alm for a variety purposes.

* Native American culture has always had tobacco as a tool for ritual, social, religious and spiritual purposes.

Native Americans use the inner bark, young leaves, pitch, and twigs of white Pine for herbal remedies.

* Wild Yam has always been used both as medicine and food.

Bone Density:

* Alfalfa- A food additive that is used for a variety of medicinal purposes. You should avoid any auto-immune condition.

* Ashwagandha-The whole plant can be used in many different treatments. This plant is dangerous and should not be taken lightly.

Chasteberry is a tea made of berries and flowers. Chasteberry is not recommended for pregnant women or those who are nursing.

Bowel problems and disease:

* American Ginseng can also be used in teas and other tonics.

* The root and leaves are made into tea by boiling them, and the washes are then used to wash their skin.

* Boneset Tea - This is tea made from dried leaf. It can be dangerous and have side effects, so please use caution.

* Cascara Sagrada-Tea made from dried bark. The bark must first be fully dried and aged before being used.

* Chokecherry -- One of the most important herbs in Native American Medicine was

* Elderberries can be eaten whole when fully ripe.

Garcinia Cambogia is a fruit-rind extract that can be used in a number of ways. It is not recommended by people suffering from diabetes, dementia, and pregnant or lactating women.

* Ginger root can also be used to season and treat ailments around the world.

* Green Tea - This is the Camellia Sinensis tea that's made only from Camellia Sinensis plants leaves. It has many health benefits.

* Peppermint is a long-standing herbal medicine ingredient that has been used for its soothing and numbing qualities, as well flavoring. This product should be avoided by infants and children.

* Psyllium Seed Husk: A high-fiber supplement traditionally used to aid in digestion.

* Sweetflag: The sweetflag has a long history in medicinal use in herbal cultures.

* Valerian Root: Valerian Root has long been used as a healing herb in ancient Greece and Rome.

* Wheat Grass- This grass is used to treat many medical conditions. It has been cultivated over the past decades.

Breast Milk

* Fennel has leaves, seeds and roots that can be used to make medicine and food.

* Milkweed: Milkweed is a plant that can be used as a medicine and food. It was also used in the making of ropes, strings and coarse cloth. Milkweed can cause poison if it is not prepared properly.

* Star anise (a small tree whose fruits have a licorice like taste) has been used in medicinal treatments for a long time.

* Sumac: Sumac was sacred to some peoples. It was used for medicine and food.

Breast discomfort:

* Partridgeberry, a plant used to treat a variety ailments, is especially effective for women.

* Native Americans used wild ginger root as a spice and medicinal plant.

Bones broken into pieces

* Buffaloberry is a fruit that can be eaten and used for herbal remedies. Overindulgence can result in severe consequences, including death.

Native Americans use the inner bark, young leaves, pitch, and twigs of white Pine for herbal remedies.

Bronchial Infections & Issues

* While bloodroot is most commonly used to treat digestive problems and respiratory issues, it can also serve as a topical treatment. We now know that it is dangerous and that the FDA has declared it to be hazardous.

* Cardinal Flower leaves, Cardinal Flower roots, and leaf tea were used both internally and externally.

* Echinacea Kreosote Bush: The roots were chewed.

* Eucalyptus Teas and Ointments for a Wide Range of Uses

* Ginger root is used around the world as a seasoning or medicine.

* Horehound can both be used internally and externally. Peptic ulcer and gastritis sufferers should avoid using it.

* Teas, tonics, salves, and flowers containing horsemint leaf and flowering stems can be used to treat a wide variety of ailments. It is best to avoid it for pregnant women.

Kola nuts are used in traditional herbal and spiritual treatments. You should not use it if you're pregnant or nursing.

* Marshmallow Root: This root has long been used as a food and medicine.

* Licorice Roots are used in food as a flavoring or herbal remedy.

* Plantain — Considered sacred by the ancient Saxons as one of the nine sacred plant species, it has a long history and is used as an alternative to traditional medicine.

* Pleurisyroot has been used long-term to treat a variety respiratory problems.

* Rabbit Tobacco -- Many Indians believed this to possess mystical or magical properties.

* Senna is a large group of flowering plants that can be useful in a variety remedies. Native

Americans have used Slippery Elm in a variety of ways.

* For various ailments, you can use teas, poultices, or oils made with spearmint both internally and externally.

* Wheat Grass- This grass is used to treat many medical conditions. It has been cultivated over the past decades.

Native Americans use the inner bark, young leaves, pitch, and twigs of white Pine for herbal remedies.

* The dried bark of wild black cherry was often used in syrups and teas to treat different ailments.

* Wild garlic is used in culinary and medicinal dishes throughout history.

* Wild Onion's use as a medicine or food has a long history.

* Wormwood-The flowers and leaves from this plant were dried and collected for use as tonics.

Abrasions:

* Arnica is not recommended for use topically. It can be poisonous if consumed internally.

* Broom Snakeweed leaves and roots can be used to make steam treatments, teas, or poultices.

* Catnip-The leaves of the catnip tree are used to make salves for wound treatment.

* Evening primrose - Decoctions were used in internal and exterior illnesses, and for nutritional or medical purposes.

* Rabbit Tobacco -- Many Indians believed this to possess mystical or magical properties.

* Sage has been used to cook for thousands upon thousands of years. Like other culinary herbs, it is considered a digestive aid as well as an appetite stimulant.

* For various ailments, you can use teas, poultices, or oils made with spearmint both internally and externally.

* St John's Wort is an herb that is most commonly used in antidepressant. However, it also has other medical benefits.

Native Americans use the inner bark, young leaves, pitch, and twigs of white Pine for herbal remedies.

* American Indians used witchhazel extensively for their medicinal purposes.

Burns:

* While bloodroot is most commonly used to treat digestive problems and respiratory issues, it can also serve as a topical treatment. It has been declared dangerous by the FDA.

* Buck Brush is an umbrella term for a group North American shrubs, which are used in herbal medicines.

* Chokecherry -- Native American medicine used Chokecherry as medicine and food.

* The cattail is an herb that can be used as a vegetable or in internal and exterior medicine.

* Many conditions can be treated by using the cotton roots, leaves, and seed.

* Greenbriar- External and internal use of teas, salves and greenbriar.

* Lavender: Lavender has been used as a tea, balm, food, or herbal remedy since Roman times.

* Mint – These dried leaves are used in teas, foods, and in other remedies.

* Oak: The bark and acorns from the oak tree are used to treat many ailments.

Pinon: This was the Native American term for Pinon, which was widely used by Native Americans. Some tribes have called it the "tree that gives life."

* The younger pads of the pear Cactus were used by the Abrasive Native Americans to make food and tea. The mature pads were used for poultices.

* Rabbit Tobacco -- Many Indians believed it to have mystical or mystic qualities.

* Sumac: Sumac was sacred to some peoples. It was used for medicine and food.

* Western Skunk Cabbage- Native Americans use this plant's "skunky" smell for topical medicine.

* Yellow Spined Thistle was used for centuries in Native American medicine.

Cancer:

* Cat's Claw: Cat's Claw can be used in teas or tonics for more than 2000 years.

* The inner rind, pulp, and grapefruit seeds can all be used to treat internal diseases.

* Green Tea - This is the Camellia Sinensis tea that's made only from Camellia Sinensis plants leaves. It has many health benefits.

* Jiaogulan, a Chinese herb that is well-known for its anti-aging properties and many health benefits.

* Maca has always been used to supplement or for medicinal purposes.

* Oat straw was used as both a food source, and as a medical treatment since prehistoric times.

* Olive Oil, a tree crop popular in Mediterranean countries, has been used in medicine and food for hundreds of years.

* Pau d'arco has for many years been used to treat a variety if ailments.

* Poke: Although some parts of this plant are toxic to livestock and humans it has been used by Native Americans for many years as food, medicine, and fuel.

* Rosemary, a herb used in both medicine and cooking, is also known as

Red Clover has been used for many years to treat a wide range of conditions.

* Sarsaparilla has been used for many herbal treatments over the years.

* Spirulina -- Spirulina can be described as a type blue-green alga rich in vitamins and proteins.

* Sumac: Sumac was sacred to some people. It was used for medicine and food.

* Thistle, a member the daisy families, is a flowering plant that is used for medicinal purposes for more then 2,000 years.

* Wheat Grass- This grass is used to treat many medical conditions. It has been cultivated over the past decades.

* Wild garlic is used in culinary and medicinal dishes throughout history.

Chest Ache

* American Licorice- Internally chewed.

* Chokecherry -- Native American medicine used Chokecherry as medicine and food.

* Native Americans used Black Gum in pools and washes.

* Sassafras- Native Americans used this for food and medicine long before European settlers arrived.

Having children:

* Sage has been used to cook for thousands upon thousands of years. Like other culinary herbs, it is considered a digestive aid as well as an appetite stimulant.

* Star anise (a small tree whose fruits have a licorice taste) has been used in medicinal remedies for a long time.

* Wild Yam has always been used both as food and medicine.

* Wormwood-The flowers and leaves from this plant were dried and collected for use as tonics.

Work can be difficult

* Buck Brush is an umbrella term for a group North American shrubs, which are used in herbal medicines.

* Feverfew: This herb can be used for several internal medical issues. Pregnant women should not use it.

Induce Labor

* Teas, tonics and salves made from horsemint leaf and flowering stems can be used to treat a wide variety of ailments. It is best to avoid it for pregnant women.

* Partridgeberry, a plant used to treat a variety ailments, is especially effective for women.

* You can use carrots (wild and domesticated) to treat a variety ailments.

Childbirth

* Blue Cohosh root used in teas and tonics

* Fenugreek herb can be used externally and internally to treat various ailments.

* Partridgeberry, a plant used to treat a variety ailments, is especially effective for women.

* Raspberry fruits and leaves can be used to treat a wide range of illnesses.

Post-Partum Hemorrhage

* Buckwheat – The fruit seed was used to supplement herbal remedies.

* Chokecherry -- Native American medicine used Chokecherry as medicine and food.

* Fendler's Bladderpod- Crushed leaves were used externally and internally.

* Raspberry fruits and leaves can be used to treat a wide range of illnesses.

* Sumac: Sumac was sacred to some people. It was used for medicine and food.

Postpartum distress:

* Ashwagandha-The whole plant can be used in many different treatments. This plant is dangerous and should not be taken lightly.

* Dong Quai can be used to treat a number of conditions for more than a thousand years.

* Milkweed: Milkweed is a plant that can be used as a medicine and food. It was also used in the making of ropes, strings and coarse cloth. The toxic effects of milkweed if consumed internally can be fatal if it is not prepared properly.

Cholera

* Chokecherry -- Native American medicine used Chokecherry as medicine and food.

* Senna is a large group of flowering plants from the genus Senna that has been used in a variety remedies.

* Sweetflag: The sweet flag is an ancient medicinal tool in many herbal traditions.

Cholesterol (reduced).

* Boswellia -- A fragrant resin that can be used to treat many conditions. This product should be avoided by both pregnant and nursing mothers as well as children.

* Fenugreek herb can be used externally and internally to treat various ailments.

* Ginger root is used around the world as a seasoning or medicine.

* Glucomannan has been used in Asia for a very long time as a dietary supplement. It is not recommended to be used by pregnant women or those who are breastfeeding.

* The inner rind, pulp, and grapefruit seeds can all be used to treat internal diseases.

* Green Tea - This is the Camellia Sinensis tea that's made only from Camellia Sinensis plants leaves. It has many health benefits.

* Gymnema Silvestre has been used as natural diabetes medication for about 2,000 year.

* Jiaogulan, a Chinese herb that is well-known for its anti-aging properties and many health benefits.

Oat straw was used both as a food source for prehistoric humans and as a treatment for ailments.

* Psyllium Seed Husk: A high-fiber supplement traditionally used to aid in digestion.

* Native Americans used younger pads from the prickly Pear cactus for tea and food, while the mature pads were used as poultices.

* Thistle, a member the daisy families, is a flowering plant that has been used to treat a variety of ailments for over 2,000 year.

* Wild garlic is used for both medicinal and culinary purposes throughout history.

Health and Circulatory Problems

* Buckwheat – The fruit seed was used to supplement herbal remedies.

* Burdock- Both the roots and the leaves of this plant can be used externally and internally. Stay away from this plant if youre pregnant or breastfeeding.

* Dong Quai can be used to treat a number of conditions for more than a thousand years.

* Ginger root is used around the world as a seasoning or medicine.

* Ginkgo Biloba- This tree, one of the oldest on the planet, has been used to provide food and medicinal purposes for thousands of year.

* Ginsing: For thousands upon thousands of year, different specifics have been employed in herbal treatment around the globe.

* The inner rind, pulp, and grapefruit seeds can all be used to treat internal diseases.

* Lecithin, which is found in many plants, has numerous benefits for various body systems.

* Osha Native Americans highly revere OSHA for its many medicinal properties.

* Persimmons - This fruit is well-known for its long history of being used in traditional medicine and as food.

* Plantain – The ancient Saxons considered it to be one the nine sacred plant species. It has a long history of being used as an alternative medicine, dating back to antiquity.

Red Clover has long been used for many ailments.

* Rosemary, a herb, is used for medicine and cooking.

* Sarsaparilla has been used for many herbal treatments over the years.

* Sassafras, a Native American herb that Native Americans used for food and medicine before European settlers arrived.

* Wild roses of all varieties have been used for medicinal purposes for thousands ofyears.

* The dried bark of wild black cherry was used in syrups and teas to treat various diseases.

* Since thousands years, Yarrow has been used as a way to stop bleeding.

* Yellow Dock was used as traditional medicine by Native Americans.

* Yerba Mate Holly species has a long history in medicinal herbs.

Coughs:

* Allspice – Teas made of dried unripe fruits have been around for a while.

* Native Americans might smoke American Ginseng. The herb is used in teas as well as tonics.

* Boneset Tea - This is tea made from dried leaf. It is dangerous and can have side effects so be careful.

* Broom Snakeweed leaves and roots can be used to make steam treatments, teas, or poultices.

* Catnip is a herb that produces a tea with a pleasant aroma. It can be used to treat various ailments.

* Cardinal Flower leaves, Cardinal Flower roots, and leaf tea were used both internally and externally.

* Chokecherry -- Native American medicine used Chokecherry as medicine and food.

Gum and Mouth Issues

* Blue Cohosh root used in teas and tonics

* Catnip is a herb that produces a tea with a pleasant aroma. It can be used to treat various ailments.

* Fennel has leaves, seeds and roots that can be used to make medicine and food.

* Ginger root is used around the world as a seasoning or medicine.

* Teas, tonics, salves, and flowers containing horsemint leaf and flowering stems can be used to treat a variety a ailments. Avoid it for pregnant women.

* Lemon balm has been used since the Middle Ages as a soothing herb.

* Licorice Roots are used in food as a flavoring ingredient and herbal remedy.

* Rooibos – Rooibos Tea is used for several conditions.

* Savory: An aromatic herb used in folk medicines and as a flavoring agent.

* Star anise (a small tree whose fruits have a licorice like taste) has been used in medicinal treatments for a long time.

* Sweetflag: The sweetflag has a long history in medicinal use in herbal cultures.

* Valerian Root: Valerian Root has long been used as a healing herb in ancient Greece and Rome.

* The dried bark of wild black cherry was used in syrups and teas to treat various diseases.

* Wild garlic is used for medicinal purposes and culinary purposes throughout history.

* Wild Lettuce is a North American native that was traditionally used to sedate nervous conditions.

* Wild Yam has always been used both as food and medicine.

Dysentery

* The black raspberry root and leaves can be made into tea or chewed.

* Buckwheat – The fruit seed was used to supplement herbal remedies.

* A wide range of ailments have been treated by cotton roots, leaves, and seed.

Garcinia Cambogia (or fruit rind) can be used for a number of different purposes.

Diabetes.

* Geranium -- A scented Geranium that can be used to treat a wide range of conditions.

Guarana can have many of the same effects that coffee, because it contains caffeine.

* Honeysuckle – For thousands upon years honeysuckle is used in traditional herbal remedies.

Ear infections and Earache

* Geranium -- A geranium that smells like geranium and is used in teas to treat many ailments.

* Mullein is an herb-like tobacco plant, which has a long history as a medicinal remedy.

* Passion Flower: Native Americans used this flower for many years, and European colonists later adopted it. Passionflower should never be consumed if you're pregnant, nursing, or otherwise ill.

* Plantain – Plantain is considered by the ancient Saxons one of the nine sacred plant, and has a long history for alternative medicine. It dates back to antiquity.

* Native Americans used wild ginger root as a spice and medicinal plant.

Eczema

* Elderberries are ripe elderberries and can be used to make herbal remedies or as a snack.

* Fenugreek herb can be used externally and internally to treat various ailments.

* Marshmallow Root: This root has long been used as a food and medicine.

* Plantain – Considered sacred by the ancient Saxons as one of the nine sacred plant species, it has a long history and is used as an alternative to traditional medicine.

Red Clover has been used for many years to treat a wide range of conditions.

* Wild yams have been traditionally used for both medicine and food.

* American Indians used witchhazel extensively for their medicinal purposes.

* Yarrow has long been used to stop bleeding.

Scratching:

* Feverwort can both be used internally and externally.

* Mint - These dried leaves are used in teas, foods, and in other remedies.

* Pennyroyal is used for treating medical issues and pests. Women who are pregnant should

not use pennyroyal. Overdosing with this herb can lead to death.

* Stoneseed seed can be used for a number of medical conditions.

* Yellow Dock was used as traditional medicine by Native Americans.

Jaundice

* Boswellia -- A fragrant resin that has been used in the treatment of many conditions. It is not recommended for use by children, pregnant women, and mothers who are breastfeeding.

* Senna is a large group of flowering plants from the genus Senna that has been used in a variety remedies.

Joints and Other Joint Questions

* Devil's Claw (Internally, it's used to make teas and tonics. Externally, it's used to make poultices. This product is not recommended for pregnant women.

* Feverwort is an herb that can be used externally and internally.

* Ginger root is used around the world as a seasoning or medicine.

Kidney Stones

* Alfalfa- A food additive that is used for a variety of medicinal purposes. You should avoid any auto-immune condition.

* Buck Brush is an umbrella term for a group North American shrubs, which are used in herbal medicines.

* The cattail is an herb that can be used as a vegetable or in internal and exterior medicine.

* Dandelion plants can be used as both medicinal and food ingredients.

* Devil's Claw (Internally, it's used to make teas and tonics. Externally, it's used to make poultices. This product is not recommended for pregnant women.

* For many years, goldenrod has been used to treat a variety of ailments.

* The inner rind, pulp, and grapefruit seeds can all be used to treat internal diseases.

* Juniper is a herb that can be used internally and externally. Because of the risk of miscarriage, pregnant women should avoid this herb.

* Oak-Acorns and bark can be used to treat various illnesses.

Menopause:

* Alfalfa- A food additive that is used for a variety of medicinal purposes. You should avoid any auto-immune condition.

* Black Cohosh Tea - Teas made with the roots of the plant have been used to treat many ailments.

Chasteberry is a tea made of berries and flowers. Chasteberry should not be consumed by pregnant or breastfeeding mothers.

* Dong Quai can be used to treat a number of conditions for more than a thousand years.

* Maca has always been used to supplement or for medicinal purposes.

Red Clover has been used to treat a wide range of conditions for many years.

Sage has been used in culinary arts for thousands upon thousands of year.

* Star anise (a small tree whose fruits have a licorice like taste) has been used in medicinal treatments for a long time.

* St John's Wort is an herb that is most commonly used in antidepressant. However, it also has many medical applications.

* Wild Yam has always been used both as medicine and food.

Cramps and pain during menstruation

* Allspice – Teas made of dried unripe fruits have been around for a while.

* Black Cohosh Tea - Teas made with the plant's roots were used to treat many ailments.

* Dong Quai can be used to treat a number of conditions for more than a thousand years.

* Ginger root is used around the world as a seasoning or medicine.

* Hibiscus: There are many varieties and uses for hibiscus in traditional herbal medicine. This has been the case since Roman times.

* Horehound is an herb that can be used externally and internally. Peptic ulcer and gastritis sufferers should avoid using it.

* Osha Native Americans highly revere OSHA due its wide variety of medicinal properties.

* Partridgeberry, a plant used to treat a variety ailments, is especially effective for women.

* Peppermint is a long-standing herbal medicine ingredient that has been used for its soothing and numbing qualities, as well flavoring. This product should be avoided by infants and children.

www.ingramcontent.com/pod-product-compliance
Lightning Source LLC
Chambersburg PA
CBHW050023130526
44590CB00042B/1856